JOY OF MARRIAGE

by Clayton C. Barbeau

WINSTON PRESS

Library of Congress Catalog Card Number: 80-51111
ISBN: 0-86683-759-0 (previously ISBN: 0-03-057841-8)
Printed in the United States of America
5 4 3

Winston Press, Inc.
430 Oak Grove
Minneapolis, Minnesota 55403

JOY OF MARRIAGE

CONTENTS

TO MYRA,

who has freely shared herself and generously accepted me through all these years and whose presence is in the best of these pages;

TO MICHAEL, AMY, ROSE-MARIE, MARGARET, MARK, DANIEL, JENNIFER, AND CHRISTOPHER,

our sons and daughters, whose enjoyment of life constantly enriches our own; and

TO THE MANY PERSONS AROUND THE COUNTRY

who shared their concerns, their problems, their insights, and asked that this book be written.

CHAPTER I

MARRIAGE:
THE CREATIVE
CHALLENGE

M arriage is an art form, the most challenging and complex of all the works a human being can be inspired to create. Unlike painting, poetry, the novel, architecture, or any other of the forms in which the essential creative element of our human nature finds expression, man-the-maker cannot lay down the tools of this art form, step back, and pronounce the work complete. The creators live within and are components of their ongoing creative work. The work of human art that is marriage is a living reality, and the married are personally caught up in its dynamism. Husbands and wives might, as other artists do, reflect upon the present state of the creation, seek objectively to consider its qualities, make resolves for improving the work; but they themselves remain part of the subject of the work itself. A marriage can never be viewed as an object—a thing that can be manipulated—for it is the unique, never-to-be-duplicated relationship of two persons, two human beings who cannot, save in a crime against humanity, be reduced to mere things.

Unlike most other works of human art, the creation of marriage is, of its essence, a collaborative work. Wife and

bring to their wedding themselves in all their
ᴜness: their personal histories, their bodies,
heir fears, their yearnings for happiness, their
es and illusions, their dreams, their infirmities
ᴜkes them distinct from all other persons now
born, or ever to be born. Their uniqueness as
persons, the essential differences between them is the
"stuff" out of which they are to bring forth that work of art
which is their common task: their marriage. Believing that
with each other they can have a fuller life, experience a
wholeness neither could know alone, they commit themselves to each other in a mutual work which, almost para-
doxically, has for its ultimate and ideal goal what too many
seem to believe has been accomplished at its outset: their
wedding in love.

There are influential, if not profound, voices being
heard today declaiming in all the media that marriage is an
outmoded institution; that the monogamous marriage en-
tailing sexual fidelity and lifelong union is an unattainable
ideal in our age; or worse, it is old-fashioned and unsophisticated. Books retailing this message have made mil-
lionaires of their authors, and no television talk show seems
able to schedule a week without a guest who solemnly or
flippantly enunciates the same message. One talk show permitted a guest artist to buttress his opinions as "expert"
because he had been married so many times. The constant
reiteration of attacks, both open and subtle, upon the marriage commitment creates an atmosphere of opinion, a climate of attitudes that is capable of weakening strong marriage relationships and proving fatal to those already
weakened by more basic problems. Like an invisible gas,
such attitudes sap the strength, cause a loss of nerve, breed
personal doubts and fears, and in a dozen ways corrode the
will to create an exciting, vibrant marriage.

Of course, such atmospheric pressures have less influence upon those couples who are more informed about the
realities of marriage. Indeed, when a couple has entered
marriage with due reflection upon what their commitment

entails—that it is the mutual lifework of lovemaking—and has given a full commitment of their wills to the task, they are immune to much of the broadcast nonsense. Their response to the so-called marriage expert, whose credentials are his multiple divorce decrees, is a good healthy laugh. Their reaction to those who counsel that a healthy marriage should be open to adulterous liaisons is sad bewilderment that such advice can be given—and accepted. They see it as a pitiful inability to understand the rich fullness that a life of fidelity can bring; and they believe that only tragedy awaits those troubled souls who seek such a solution to their problems.

Unfortunately, we seem to have few truly vibrant and living marriages created in our society. That this is so, and that the divorce rate is so high, is offered by some as testimony to the fact that the lifelong creative work of marriage is an impossible commitment in our day. Such an argument, based on marital failures, becomes a factor in causing more failures.

In this book, we will be treating of the qualities of mature marriages—marriages of fifteen or more years. We will be specifically concerned with helping marriages which, in these middle years, face communications problems, emotional distresses and other tensions that are more common at this stage than earlier in the relationship. It is the aim of this work to provide some assistance to those who wish to breathe new life into their marriage, to make a change for the better in communications, to add vitality and greater pleasure to their living together. But no marriage lives in isolation, and it is well for us to consider at the outset, if only in a general way, some of the basic thinking about marriage prevalent today.

Sadly enough, many marriages are false from the start. This is quite obvious in the case of the couple who announced that they had agreed to marry and: "After six months, if it hasn't worked out, we'll get an amicable divorce." Anyone who has ever reflected upon the mystery of the marriage commitment would not be surprised to learn that this marriage did not even last out its six months' probationary period before it had become yet another divorce statistic. Many false marriages are less obvious, but surely the majority of teen-age marriages fall into this category. About forty percent of all brides in America are between fifteen and eighteen years of age. It is estimated that the divorce rate for teen-age marriages is three to four times higher than that for marriages contracted later in life. If we removed these figures from our statistics on divorce, our entire picture of the marriage/divorce ratio in our society would be drastically altered, and one of the chief props of the "marriage is dying" platform would be removed.

It is not the chronological age of the couple that is important in regard to false marriages, but the fact that their decision to marry is ill-considered, based on immature reasoning, and often compounded by unrealistic expectations. Ulterior motives, such as pregnancy, the desire to be adult and/or free from parents, the pressure of peers, or any other problem to which marriage seems the solution, may be prompting the decision. Such motives for marrying are completely irrelevant to the reality of the marriage mystery. Built on false foundations, most such marriages collapse within a few years, torn apart by the tensions which, in a true marriage, are the energies for creativity in the relationship.

Marital vows given for ulterior motives are not reserved to teen-agers, however. Immature reasons leading to false marriages know no age limits. The man in his forties who, in a whirlwind courtship, wooed and wed the woman in her mid-thirties—the first marriage for each of them—had come to the conclusion before meeting her that it was time to settle down. The "dating game" with its ploys and stratagems had palled; he was becoming increasingly aware of his age. The woman saw it as her last chance to "catch a man," to escape being an old maid, and to have the child for which she yearned. Such a couple, grasping at marriage as a personal life raft offering rescue from their sea of inner doubts and fears, have also entered a false marriage. One baby and four years later, the marriage hovers on the brink of divorce.

Nor is the basically false marriage commitment warded off by the premarital cohabitation which an estimated five percent of couples choose. One such couple in their mid-twenties, having lived together for over two years, got married because, as he put it: "She wants to be married and we may as well." During the month of their first wedding anniversary, she filed for divorce. She, it seems, had expected marriage to make a change in him.

When we speak of false marriages, we are not referring to the legality or the binding nature of their commitment so far as the courts of Church or State are concerned, but to the attitudes of the persons involved, their true motives, the inner conditions and external pressures to which they are submitting. When the marital commitment flows from sources unrelated to the partner, when the other person involved is seen as the means of solving a personal problem, when marriage itself is viewed as the solution to a problem, we have serious reason to doubt the authenticity of the marital commitment. When the marriage vow is seen as a mere formality imposed by outside legal authority, rather than an expression of the deepest personal commitment of the will to the good of the other, when marriage is considered an end in itself and not the beginning of a lifelong creative work, to that degree the vow and the marriage is unauthentic and falsified. When the "yes" is made conditional to open or hidden reservations, the marriage is to that degree crippled at the outset. When persons get married thinking of it as a goal reached, an "institution" entered, rather than the beginning of a long, arduous, at times exhilarating, at times exhausting, life's work, then they enter marriage with their eyes closed and one of the many pitfalls on the landscape of reality may claim their marriage relationship as its victim.

Some marriages that have gotten off to a false start do in fact recover. These most often involve one marriage partner who was not diluting his or her commitment, who did give authentic response to the other and to the future with the other. As the couple's unity is threatened, this spouse shows such constancy, such courage in loving, such strength of will in crisis that the other is helped to mature. A bridge is built over the chasm, and the other is led across it to a truer appreciation of marriage. Because of the one, the other's commitment now finds truer ground. The reason for getting married is no longer the reason for staying married: better reasons have been discovered through the help of the spouse.

We can be grateful, as can our children, that in our time much attention is focused upon the task of preparing our young people for marriage. Not only do most schools offer family life education courses, but parents themselves are more aware of their personal responsibility for the attitudes of their children toward sex, marriage, and family life. Some Churches now require premarital psychological testing and counseling for teen-agers seeking marriage. Some state legislatures are being urged to impose such counseling requirements on teen-agers applying for marriage licenses.

While all such efforts are welcomed as steps to help reduce the personal suffering and social damage occasioned by divorce among the young, we find a growing phenomenon in our time: marriages which, after fifteen to thirty years of shared life, are in the midst of a divorce crisis or are already broken by divorce. Many of these, undoubtedly, were marriages that never overcame their false start. In some of these situations, the couple have maintained their marriage for a number of years for the same ulterior motive that prompted it, or have manufactured new ulterior motives. Those who married to "give the baby a name," may have remained together "for the sake of the children." Persons who married to enhance their social or economic status may have remained married because divorce would jeopardize that newfound status. Some, it must be said, stick to their "bad bargain" (what a travesty of marriage that term evokes!) out of sheer inertia. Still, even after enduring for some years, a false marriage can collapse when the initial motive evaporates—the child is now grown, financial reverses have been suffered, divorce is no longer a social stigma among their peers, or a third party has overcome the inertia.

Some partners to such long-lived false marriages are capable of maintaining an exterior facade of such quality as to be considered authentic even by their spouses. There is a letter on my desk from the feminine half of a marriage of thirty years duration. On their most recent anniversary, the letter relates, her husband announced: "I don't love you. I don't think I ever loved you. I want a divorce." Despite her almost total shock, he informed her that there was nothing she could do to change his mind; there was another woman he wanted to marry. He revealed that he had married for less than authentic reasons, that for years he had maintained a facade, played the loving role so skillfully that theirs was generally considered an ideal marriage. He had found the situation comfortable. He was genuinely loved by his wife, but he had no strong reciprocal loving commitment. The entrance into his life of an attractive enough outside force had overcome his inertia.

The shock of such news is not limited to the spouse. Anv such marital collapse shakes other marriages. A man involved in premarriage education within his church said: "In the last year my wife and I have received news of divorce from six different couples among our closest friends, people our age, married twenty years or more. One of these couples we had thought of as an inspiration to us, a truly ideal marriage. It was as if someone died. We were sick about it for weeks. It frightened us. We thought that if they couldn't succeed, weren't able to cope, how could we?"

Nor does the phenomenon stop with the middle-aged. A recent Sunday supplement carried an article examining the increasing numbers of divorcing grandparents. A part of the explanation offered for this syndrome was that many of these couples, having related to one another solely as father and mother of their children, found it difficult when thrown back upon the husband/wife relationship. With twenty to thirty years of life expectancy still ahead for them, the argument went, they were choosing to divorce and seek fulfillment elsewhere. Like many Sunday supplement explorations of such matters, the argument—reiterated by prominent commentators whose research should be more thorough—was that the new development was due to the extended life expectancy we enjoy that our grandparents did not. In fact, the statistical life expectancy of such couples today is not much more than a few months longer than that enjoyed by couples the same age a century or more ago. Today's supposed extended life expectancy is based upon the fact that a century ago so many babies were stillborn or died of childhood diseases that are now eradicated. Actually, persons reaching middle age today have a statistical life expectancy not too different from that of their great-grandparents.

The erroneous "extended life expectancy" argument runs a close second to the divorce statistics as proof that monogamous marriages no longer meet the needs of contemporary man. Both arguments have done much mischief in the way of creating the bad climate of opinion regarding the chances of success in creating a marriage. In actual fact, about eighty percent of those divorced remarry and make a success of their second attempt at a monogamous, permanent relationship. The slow learners or the incurably immature, who make divorce a habit, merely cloud the issue of how accurate our marriage/divorce statistics really are in giving us some clear grasp of the ratio of enduring marriages to failed marriages.

Indeed, many and various are the explanations being offered for the breakdown of long-term marriages. The "male menopause," the breakdown or blurring of traditional marital roles, the heavier psychological and emotional burdens the marriage relationship is said to bear today, the isolation of the nuclear family, the contemporary stress upon sexual fulfillment; these are only a random sampling of reasons being proferred. In spite of the fact that ninety-five percent of our marriageable population do, in fact, marry, some authors go beyond seeking causes—whether glandular, psychological, or sociological—and merely declare that marriage as we have known it is an outmoded tradition soon to be bypassed by some more up-to-date arrangement.

Extrapolating from the present divorce system, which permits successive polygamy, one writer prophesied that the marriage of the future would institutionalize divorce as the normal course of marriage. He suggested that a man would take one wife for his sexual companion in younger years, replace her with another to be the mother of his children, and replace her with a third whom he desired as his companion in old age. The male chauvinism of this suggestion—that women are mere replaceable parts in a man's life—seemed to escape the notice of the reviewers of this best seller.

The small minority of persons cohabiting without benefit of marriage commitment usually dismiss the lack of a vow with words about their personal relationship not needing legal sanction or a "mere scrap of paper." As far as can be determined by surveys, however, theirs are usually quite traditional monogamous relationships. Indeed, one such couple of my acquaintance has been secretly married for over three years, but fear loss of status with their peers if the word leaks out.

Some popular books of recent years have extolled the marriage which is open to "extra-marital" or "co-marital" sexual relationships, thereby baptizing with a new name the ancient practice of adultery. Their cautions that such relationships should be mutually agreed to in honest dialogue with the spouse, entered upon with mature reflection and some ethical sensitivity, do little to deter the partner who is teetering on the brink of adultery. In fact, the books serve to help the partner so inclined to convict the other of being immature, closed in, and unsophisticated. More, they can cause problems where none before existed. Within the past month one young man, married six years and in love with his wife, sought counsel about whether he should have sexual relations with a woman in his office who was single and, apparently, inviting. Asked why, since he was in love with his wife and happily married, he was considering the matter, he responded that he had read some books that said it was all right and that it might even improve his marriage.

Such writings often enough pay solemn lip service to the marital contract, but are quite unclear as to what constitutes the essence of that contract. If a couple making a commitment of marriage are not fundamentally committing themselves to be the exclusive sexual partners of one another, faithful through the vicissitudes of the future, then the critics of "legalism" are quite right. Who needs a "scrap of paper" or a public announcement to share a bedroom for just as long as each finds it personally convenient?

If the technological view of the world, as so much matter capable of being manipulated to our individual gratification, has now been applied to human persons—as in the futurist's notion of marriage—it has also wreaked its havoc on many marriages through the proliferation of sex manuals. In later pages of this work we shall discuss the matter of sexual communication in marriage in some detail. Here it suffices to take note of the fact that marriage manuals are too often "mechanics manuals." They offer to the technological man a technology of sex: some even have titles proclaiming that they are teaching "technique." It was left to our era to reduce the most sublime of human expressions of love to a matter of the proper lubrication and manipulation of anatomical parts, the juxtapositioning of genital organs, all in the name of (shades of the industrial revolution!) sexual "adjustment." The very popularity of each season's new manuals is a measure of the failure of last year's best seller to deliver on its promise of increased marital happiness. Indeed, not only do such works fail to help most marriages, they often become a factor in impeding the growth of some. Like so many of the explanations and solutions we are offered, the "mechanics manuals" often become contributory factors to conjugal disharmony, marital unrest, and even marriage failure.

We've touched upon these negative factors regarding marriage in our society because there is simply no way any existing marriage can escape their influence, whether it be one now enjoying its honeymoon or celebrating its twentieth anniversary.

In the chapters that follow, we shall explore some of the problems of the middle years of marriage in a realistic fashion. The theme of marital fidelity and the meaning of commitment and freedom in regard to the marriage relationship will be examined. Because many find themselves, after years of living together, caught up in the same futile arguments, we will offer some observations on ways of breaking out of this stalemated situation and give some indications of the creative uses of conflict. Since it is not atypical that a marriage relationship can "plateau out" into a flat routine of functional and sterile living together, ways of moving our marriages onto new levels of awareness will be discussed. The sexuality of the middle-aged husband and wife, and the deepening of their communication of love at this crucial period of their lives is another of the themes to be treated. In presenting these observations, no pretense is made of having the only, or all, or even most of the insights capable of enriching a marriage. What is being offered, however, is gleaned from the author's twenty-odd years of marriage, as well as a dozen years of involvement in marriage education and counseling work. It was initially begun in answer to requests from many couples around the country who are undergoing the growing pains of the middle years and wish to better the quality of their relationship.

The crucial starting place for this endeavor, and the basis for all that follows, is the recognition by the couple that their marriage is very literally of their own making. If every individual born into this world is unique, never to be duplicated, then every marriage is also unique. There is no marriage on earth that is quite like any other marriage that has ever been or will be or is now on earth. Each marriage is the creation of the couple involved; it is their original work of art.

Couples not conscious of this fundamental truth about

marriage become victims of their ignorance. Couples refusing to accept responsibility for this labor of love become victims of their irresponsibility. And we have no lack of such victims around us. There are those who think of marriage as a "given," something that "occurs" at a wedding ceremony. Thinking of marriage as an institution they inhabit rather than a temple they build, such couples expect marriage to have a power of its own. "Our marriage isn't working out," or "It was a good marriage for a time, but it has changed" are typical comments of persons who think marriage is something exterior to themselves, an "it" rather than an "us." Many marriages have become long-term imprisonments for husbands and wives because such an attitude inhibits their growth. Not recognizing their own creative role, they put forth little or no energy to change the situation. In some cases they bewail their solitary confinement without recognizing that they are the possessors of the key to freedom and a new life in the relationship.

Some, aware that growth and change are possible, use their energies in seeking to work a change in their partners by prayer and precept, and are nagged by the unhappy thought that their best efforts always seem frustrated. Their sober attempts to enlighten the other have themselves become part of the same routine of daily clichés, now even lacking the emotional charge once supplied by the unexpected turn of phrase or insult.

We hope some of the insights in this work will be of help to these couples as well as to those others who are more consciously, more successfully, creating their marriages. The beginning of that creative task is to see it as such, and to be aware that we live in the marriage we have ourselves created. If we are unhappy with it, find the tones too dark, the texture too rough or too smooth, only we, with the help of our collaborator in this work, can change them. Equally important to this acceptance of personal responsibility for change and growth in our marriage is the awareness that our first step toward such new life begins with some creative change in ourselves, not in some immediate demand for change in our partner.

Change in our partner may be crucial, may be absolutely necessary. But if all our previous attempts to get through to the other have failed, it may be because we have failed to appreciate that change does not often occur as a response to a demand for change; it is not wrought by submission of a requisition slip. Most often it can be brought about as a response from our partner to a creative change that has taken place in ourselves.

Having set aside these two erroneous notions—that one is a passive victim of marriage rather than its creator, and that the creative action is directed first toward one's spouse rather than one's self—we yet need to ask ourselves what it is that this creative art is meant to produce. As stated at the outset, there is no way in which we can objectify marriage. It is not a "thing" we are creating. There is no point at which we can stop and say with pride: "We've finished our marriage, isn't it beautiful?" Our creative activity is devoted to the constant nourishing of an ongoing relationship which, through an ever-increasing intimacy of body and spirit, helps each of the partners grow in the freedom of personhood, and grow together in an incomparable unity. It is a labor of love that the truly married engage in until they are parted by death.

Instead of worrying about contracted "rights" and "obligations"—as some legalistic-minded current thinkers on marriage would have us do—the partners in a living marriage are less concerned about "my rights" and "your duties" than they are about "our marriage." They seek to express their love through attentiveness to the other's emotional, spiritual, and bodily needs. All actions, all gifts of time and service and material things are, for those involved in a living marriage, seen as but imperfect symbols of the gift of themselves to each other. Such persons learn from the experience of it that such total giving of self, when it is mutual, sees them enriched not merely with the gift of the other, but of the other enriched and more beautifully re-created by their own selves. This experience is one of the more delightful paradoxes, one of the greater mysteries of human existence. It leads to the continuing creation of

new expressions of their appreciation, their wonder, their
abiding concern for one another. The living marriage is
one in which lovemaking is continual, and which continually makes more love.

There are those who grow older and harder because they
have been the only gift-giver in the marriage. Disappointed, unappreciated, they lose their creative élan and
take to protecting their own interests in an increasingly
bitter or estranged marriage. Whatever the reason for the
loss of reciprocity—if it was ever truly there—the life is
slowly draining out of the marriage. Seldom is it one partner alone who is looking back nostalgically to the early days
of the marriage and sorrowing at its present impoverished
state in contrast to those halcyon days. Such couples can
often be seen on the much talked about "second honeymoon," each hoping these few days alone will bring back
the lost ecstasy. Too often it contributes little but disappointment and furthers the sense of hopelessness.

The creative élan is not something back in our past marital history. We cannot retrace our steps to discover that
vital spark necessary to rekindling the flames of our love.
The beginning step toward creating a living marriage is not
a step backwards at all. We do not look to our honeymoon
days, or past romantic visions of the other, and try to evoke
these in today's context. The whirlwind European tour, the
long-promised Bahama cruise, may for a few days create
the illusion of pleasure in one another's company, but often
enough all that is happening is happening outside of the
couple, distracting them from themselves, helping them
ignore their unhappiness through exterior activities. The
first moments of repose, the first days of return, find them
in their marital relationship right back where they always
were. The more they hoped in the efficacy of the second
honeymoon, the more severe is their disappointment.

The efficacious second honeymoon is the one that begins with an inner pilgrimage, a journey of the spirit in
which we reflect upon the sources of personal discontent,
the true state of my feelings toward myself, toward the
other, toward our marriage. To what degree am I myself

responsible for the very unrest, the dissatisfaction, which I feel? Often enough my dissatisfaction with my spouse may very well be a displacement of a very real dissatisfaction with myself. If I feel unhappy with myself, it will be nearly impossible for me to offer a vital, happy self to the other.

Many marriage counselors stress the need for all of us to take some time for "selfing"—doing those things which make *me* feel happier, healthier, more accomplished. Such advice often seems to run counter to our early training against being selfish and toward serving others. But selfing —taking time for one's personal needs, whether these be for privacy, for swimming, for the enjoyment of a part-time job or a hobby, or an evening course—has no overtones of selfishness when it is done in order to insure that personal growth in mental and physical health and a sense of general well-being basic to joying in life. Indeed, the person who has a healthy self-respect, a healthy love of self, is all the more capable of being that much more a creatively loving marriage partner. It is essentially myself I offer as a gift to the other. The time and energy that I devote to selfing is time and energy that benefits all my relationships with others, but most crucially my relationship with that other whose life is enriched by my total gift of self.

But if the move toward change and growth in our marriages must begin with self, the creative impulse ought not to end there. The exploration of that inner territory of self may be crucial, but it is the prelude and the ongoing accompaniment to the re-discovery of the other. In all too many marriages, the partners seem to have fallen into the belief that they "know" one another. After all, they've lived with one another all these years. There is nothing new to be discovered about the other. Such beliefs run counter to the reality of human existence: that no one of us can ever fully be known by another, that we are ultimately mysteries even to ourselves. Each day there is something new to be learned from the other who has added another day to his history and, perhaps, changed his mind, if not his heart about something.

In all too many marriages, the wife is the last to know of

her husband's virtues, let alone his vices. One survey taken in the midwest showed over fifty percent of the housewives interviewed were unable to give their husband's job title or any description at all of what he did at work. And how many husbands could immediately provide their wife's present dress size or what book she read last? Not that these are important details in themselves, but they can be revelatory of a state of mind which is basically inattentive to the other-as-other. If such superficial matters of information are unknown to the spouse, what about the deeper, more significant movements of the other's thoughts and feelings?

The wife of twenty-two years who says "I didn't know anything was seriously wrong," as she tells of her husband's departure to marry another woman, might possibly have known had she been paying loving attention to him. The astonished husband, who received a call from his wife stating that she had already moved out and was phoning from the lawyer's office, blurts: "I don't know why! I didn't think we were having any great problems." He's announcing that he hasn't paid attention to what she might think were great problems.

To begin anew our response to the creative challenge that is marriage, we do well to look at the reality of the other-as-other, as he or she is now. The look must not be clinical, analytical, so much as reflective, appreciative, an opening up of oneself to this other as if he or she is a new person who has walked into one's life today.

The early days of life together were charged with all the exhilarating power of erotic love at its most vigorous. The ecstasy—the "being beside oneself," the "outflowing to the other"—which marked the earliest days was an almost involuntary response to the goodness, the beauty, the truth of this other person whose presence made all the difference in the world. We paid such close attention to one another that we were capable of saying: "That's what I thought you were thinking," and "I knew you'd call. We must have ESP." In a sense we were enjoying extrasensory perception of each other. Our attention to the other was so keenly honed, the other was so much at the center of our concerns, that we were receiving every slightest flicker of eyelid, every subtle change in eye color, the minutest tingle of facial muscle. If we thought that all of our life together would be lived at such a high pitch of intensity, such illusions have been followed by disillusion. But there is no need to sigh for the bygone days when such attentiveness to the other was so compulsive, and often so blind. Which of us, caught up in that frenzy, ever saw the faults and did not turn them into virtues? Now, with more mature vision, we can focus our attention upon the one whose life has been joined to our own for so many years. Now, tenderly, we can try to look toward the other as he or she is, to reflect upon the other. What is he going through these days? How does her body posture, her dress, reveal her state of mind at this moment? What is his worry at present? What is her greatest need from me during this hour of our lives together? How would I describe for another person the depth of those eyes?

Time may have brought hardships, misunderstandings, sufferings of all sorts. There is no life worth living, no marriage of any length, that has not known such things. Perhaps there are things between us that still hurt. Brooding on the hurts, nursing the old wounds, is worse than noncreative: it is destructive. The attentive gaze must be looking for the more honorable scars on the other: the one he got on his arm when helping the flood victims; that on her stomach from the Caesarean; those lines about her eyes, first noticed during that awful winter when their eldest was ill—minute signs of crises bravely weathered. And happier lines, too, the tiny grooves around eyes and mouth that all those smiles have recorded, the dimple in the chin that figured so much in their early love play.

The meditation, not only upon the particularity of my spouse but upon the unique wonder of her/his existence, the shared history we've known, is the beginning of our creating in ourselves a new appreciation of who the other is, not only as other but in relation to myself. It can lead to creating a new attitude toward our marriage: a deeper understanding of what we have meant, do mean, and can mean to one another. We've reached a plateau, perhaps, and we stumbled often on the way to this flat place in our lives, but we did struggle this far together. Far from being the end of the journey, this plateau can be the place from which we begin the most wondrous years of our creative work.

Youthful energies may be waning, but so is the turbulence of adolescence with its horrific uncertainties and impossible emotional turmoil. Some of our daydreams of youth may have vanished when confronted with life's harsher realities, but our very experience of those realities has made our vision more realistic, our hopes more realizable.

Attentiveness to who we are, where we are, and what we wish to change in our relationship is that necessary reflective pause in our creative work which insures that our future shall be more consciously the work of art we intend. Such reflection upon our present relationship may, we hope, lead to a recognition that the change and growth we desire, the leaving behind of this arid place, awaits only a mutual renewal of our commitment of the will to take further creative steps into the future.

Those who decide to continue the creative task will move out from the plateau where they thought they had been stranded and continue the pilgrimage of body and soul down uneasy trails, across dry-as-dust deserts, into velvet green valleys, up new pathways to the heights of a continually fuller married life. One day, to their giddy delight, while still in process, they will discover that their youthful dream of happiness together was but an amateur's sketch alongside the vibrant colors, the rich texture, the remarkable lines of their mutual creation: their living marriage.

CHAPTER II

FIDELITY: THE CREATIVE VOW

In a group workshop on sex of which I was a participant, a young woman in her twenties announced that she and her lover had an "open relationship agreement" which permitted either of them to have outside sexual relationships. She said that she had no desire for such, she loved only him, but she confronted a problem: "I have sex with him whenever he wants, however he wants, no matter how I feel or whether or not I want to do so, because I'm afraid that if I turn him down, he'll just go to someone else and that would hurt me more than anything. But I feel like a sort of sex slave to him the way things are now."

Asked why she had opted for an open relationship agreement if she didn't really desire to exercise the option it afforded, she said, "Because we wanted to be free." When someone in the group suggested that the married women participants who had taken a vow of fidelity might actually be much freer than she was, she had difficulty comprehending this: "I don't see how committing yourself to one person spells freedom." To which one of the women replied: "Well, for one thing, it frees me from the fear that enslaves you. My husband and I have chosen to live in a sexually exclusive relationship. That means we have had a long time to work out the rhythms of our love life, our sex life. I'm not afraid that if I'm not in the mood, he might go elsewhere—or vice versa. There's nothing stopping us from doing that, of course. People do commit adultery. But if we did do that, we would know we'd broken our promise, been unfaithful."

Fidelity. The syllables once resounded with the finest echoes of humanity. The secular and sacred scriptures of the world bear testimony to the esteem in which mankind universally and during all ages held those persons whose loyalties met the tests of time and circumstances. The face of humanity at its best is revealed in those whose commitment to principle or faithfulness to persons has been sustained during times of adversity, even personal danger. We stand in wonder before such heroism. All that we call civilization is rooted in the understanding that persons are capable of keeping their freely given words, of fulfilling their promises.

The individual's oath of allegiance to a tribe or a nation, the oath of a doctor or a lawyer, the contract between two businessmen, the pledge of teammates, the promises of husband and wife—these are the warp and woof of the fabric of a livable society. Such commitments are possible because both parties can realistically expect the other to be in good faith—truthfully promising to do something within their power and ready to make every human effort to fulfill the promise. And, as society has always honored the person who keeps his promises, so it has always disdained the traitor and the liar, the one who breaks his promises for personal gain or who gives his word without intending to keep it.

Yet, in the past decade, the very word "fidelity" has become freighted with negative connotations in our society. Far from conjuring up visions of the epitome of human dignity and the highest resonances of the human spirit, the very word seems to be equated by some with notions of limitation, self-imprisonment, loss of freedom. In the specific area of marriage, it is denounced as an attempt to straitjacket the love relationship into some sort of mutual bondage.

It is understandable that in a time of great social and moral upheaval such as our own, persons will express fear of the future and withdraw from making firm commitments of any sort. The decline in the number of students making vocational commitments or planning careers, is one mark of this. The future is seen as so uncertain, the present so unstable, that they and many others opt for living "day by day," making only tentative arrangements with regard to schooling, work, or anything but the immediate future. Freedom, usually defined as freedom from long-range commitments, is the catchword of the day.

This thrust for freedom is all around us, expressing itself in sometimes bizarre fashion in the political sphere, in education, in all the arts, in the civil rights and women's movements, in the therapist's milieu—to name a few obvious examples. The most sensationalized and continuously publicized campaign for freedom has been in the area of sexual conduct. If it has been given so much attention, it is because anything to do with sex touches us all. Further, our sexuality and the expression of our sexuality are of immense importance to each of us, for we discern that our personal identity is indissolubly linked to our sexuality. I might cease to a writer, a plumber, or a lawyer; I might cease to be a student; I might cease to be sighted or two-armed or witty or ignorant; but I cannot cease to be male or female. My whole style of being-in-the-world is influenced by that link-up of myself and my sexuality; it will determine whether I shall be a mother or a father, a husband or a wife. It will determine whether the relationship with the other is heterosexual or homosexual (and all relationships with other persons, precisely because we are all sexed and cannot lay down our sexuality for an instant, are one or the other).

The sort of interest we take, the degree of insight we have into the various ideas presented to us about sex, will be heavily influenced by our own sexual education or miseducation, our own experiences of our sexuality, our current attitudes toward ourselves and the other sex. The person raised in a home where mention of sex was taboo, and any thought of sex "a dirty thought" will have a very different response to today's heavy emphasis upon sexual matters than that person whose parents gave frank answers to questions and made no "dirty secret" out of sexual information. The former may see the present era as an opportunity for breaking free of repressions or as a period of terrible and damning permissiveness against which he must fight. The latter may wonder what all the fuss is about or may worry about some of the nonsense that is passed off as "modern thought" on the matter of sexual relations. But both are confronting the same heavy emphasis upon sexual freedom in our time. It is an emphasis that gains added weight in a world where the areas of personal freedom seem to have shrunken considerably. In our conglomeratized, computerized, industrialized society, the one area of life still very largely under the control of the individual is the area of his or her sexual relationships with others.

The intense personal interest in sex, the heightened fear of the future, and the renewed thrust for human freedom all coincided in the past decade to create an avalanche of ideas and information upon sexual matters. That avalanche swept away much previous nonsense, misinformation, and sheer ignorance. Unfortunately, it also threatened to destroy the very foundation for the fullest expression of sexual love: the commitment in fidelity of a married couple. In its more frenzied aspects, the sexual freedom movement swept some of its married aspirants up into "mate-swapping," "key clubs," and the "swinging scene." Some single persons opted for cohabitational arrangements which avoided the pledge of fidelity; although, as far as surveys could ascertain, most of these, however short or long their duration, were as monogamous and sexually exclusive as any traditional marriage. Some followed the lead of various writers and "opened" their relationships—whether married or cohabitational—to third party relationships. Others sought to formalize such "openness," such nonexclusive relationships, by involving themselves in communal or group-marriage arrangements. Nearly all apologists for such arrangements found their rationale in the individual's desire to be "free," to "keep the options open."

If I have couched many of my remarks about the sexual freedom scene in the past tense, it is because there are numerous signs that the heavy emphasis placed upon sexual experimentation in the late sixties and early seventies has begun to diminish somewhat. Those bruised and battered by such experiments are nursing their wounds. Newspapers and magazines that catered to "swingers" and "swappers" are dead or are losing circulation. Many "open marriages," including some of the most famous, have ended in divorce. Psychologists and social commentators have begun to point out the pathological origins of some of the more bizarre activities of the sexual freedom cultists, including, among other possible sources of such behavior, the latent homosexuality of some wife-swappers; the fact that sexual orgies are the last place in which one is permitted to be intimate or loving with another; voyeurism; and the acting out of personal marital problems, to name but a few.

It is too bad that such voices couldn't gain a hearing amidst the wild cacaphony of the recent past. Many human beings might have been spared the suffering they went through in trying to live out the proposals of sexual theorists. Two of the most eminently qualified sexologists of our time, Virginia E. Johnson and William H. Masters, in their book *The Pleasure Bond* (Boston-Toronto: Little Brown and Company, 1974), say about those who "argue that the concept of fidelity is outmoded and must yield to a flexible arrangement which permits both husband and wife to engage in extramarital sex": "This kind of conjecturing, which totally repudiates the established principles of sexual commitment, owes less to disciplined observation of what most people require in order to live sexually effective lives than it owes to wishful fantasies about how they ought to live."

Yet it was those wishful fantasies that sent many—caught up in the *zeitqeist,* the spirit, of the last years—rushing headlong into the sexual wilderness in search of . . . What? Sexual freedom? Obviously, the young woman in the group workshop hadn't found much freedom. Nor is she alone. Dr. Robert C. Kolodny, speaking at the annual meeting of the American Association for the Advancement of Science in January of 1975, underscored this lack of freedom on the part of those who opted for the "swinging life" when he said: "People have found it more enslaving than freeing." Basing his comments on several hundred clinical interviews with couples who had come to his Reproductive Biology Research Foundation in St. Louis seeking help for sexual problems, on correspondence with troubled individuals, and on responses to his lectures in various parts of the country, he said of those opting for the sexually "free" life style: "They usually do this no more than a year and a half before giving it up." This corroborated William Masters' comment in a television interview that the couples they knew of who had opted for sexually "open" relationships either retreated from this position within a short while or obtained a divorce.

But if the sexually "open" relationship is not freeing, at least it must be "fun." Kolodny commented: "The words that show up in their conversation—like 'fatigue', 'strain', and 'effort'—indicate how difficult a life style this is to sustain. Take the references to sex out of those conversations and it sounds like they're describing life in a slave labor camp." At the same gathering at which Kolodny spoke, Dr. Amitai Etzoni, a sociologist and Columbia University professor, drew upon his interviews with 215 Greenwich Village singles and 50 Rutgers couples who had cohabited prior to getting married, and said: "Those who championed sexual free-fall are now more interested in affectionate bonding." He added: "Increasingly, the separation of sex from affection is being discovered by the avant-garde of sexual liberation to result in frustration, tension and jealousy. . . ."

Dr. Joyce Brothers, responding to a letter from a distressed woman who had become involved in a mate-swapping club in a mistaken effort to keep her marriage, said: "Whenever the emphasis is on sex without love or commitment, there is a strong likelihood that it will become boring or distasteful. According to Dr. Alfred Auerbach, clinical professor of psychiatry at the University of California's School of Medicine, only individuals with major personality problems can continue this hedonistic pursuit for a prolonged period."

We can be thankful that the aberrational aspects of the sexual freedom movement are now being pointed out in public places and even in print, but we need not believe that the law of the pendulum's swing is operative in this matter. We will not return to the days before the landslide. Nor ought we to yearn to do so. For the same avalanche that brought emotional and sexual disaster to many also wiped away much ignorance and misinformation about this vital part of our lives, knocked sex from the list of taboo topics, overcame the false notion of the sinfulness of legitimate sexual pleasure and brought many who had for years secretly suffered from sexual dysfunction into curative therapy. These are just some of the lasting benefits of the period we've just gone through.

Yet problems remain, and many of these problems continue to stem from the books and articles which repudiated the concept of fidelity as essential to marriage. Citing the millions who are seeking some guidance between the "new" morality and the "old," Masters and Johnson comment in *The Pleasure Bond:*

> These are the men and women who constitute the overwhelming majority; when they are single they know they will eventually marry, and when they get married, they do their best to stay married. But any confidence they may have had in achieving their goals cannot avoid being undermined by a society in which most of what is published in books and magazines on the subject of sex and marriage promotes the idea that, to paraphrase Ralph Waldo Emerson, a foolish fidelity is the hobgoblin of little minds. In such a climate of opinion, discussions of commitment are not likely to flourish. An entire

vocabulary shrinks; among educated people who consider themselves sophisticated, such words as loyalty and faithfulness, honor and trust, are avoided because somehow they seem suitable only for sermons. Yet all human association depends on these and other such values, and they cannot be ignored in relation to marriage. . . . As couples, the question they want answered is not what makes extra-marital sex right or wrong—but what makes it unnecessary?"

Masters and Johnson recommend that the answer to that question should seek to translate the virtues of commitment and fidelity into "functional terms, that examine how and why the sense of being mutually committed may contribute to the sexual responsiveness of both partners and the durability of their exclusive relationship."

A beginning of such an examination might be made by referring again to the girl whose lack of a mutual commitment in fidelity had, in her own words made "a sort of sex slave" out of her. That their relationship did not include a promise of sexual fidelity meant that fear was often at the root of her sexual responses to him. She was suffering in a way unknown to the married women involved in sexually exclusive relationships.

Recently I had occasion to see the same fear-based tensions destroy a relationship, this time because the woman insisted upon her freedom to engage in sexual activities with others while the man desired her exclusively. Jealousy led to quarrels, the quarrels led to her seeking solace elsewhere, and the pleasure they had once found in one another's company was displaced by increasing pain which finally separated them.

I believe it was Chesterton who first told the tale of a tiny group of seafaring people who landed on a lovely island in the springtime and built a village and planted crops. They were delighted at their good fortune and talked of the isle as paradisal. But when wintry weather came the waves of the sea rose to massive heights and buffeted the island with such force that all the villagers were forced to the treetops in order to save their lives, and from there watched the huts they had built and the gardens they had cultivated for sustenance destroyed. Many lost their lives.

When the storms passed, the remaining band commenced to build a stout wall of rocks around the island to protect themselves. Often during the years it took to build it, they were forced to the treetops to save their lives. Eventually the wall was completed, and for generations thereafter the people lived happily, dancing their joy in festivals, improving their homes, creating things of beauty.

Indeed, so protected were they for so long that only a few of the very oldest among them remembered, from stories told in their childhood, why the wall had been built. Others treated these stories as legends and some among them began to insist that the wall ought to be torn down. "It restricts our freedom," they said. "It impedes our view of the sea." "It prevents us from running into the waves, which would be most pleasurable." "It imprisons us. We are walled in." When a few of the older people tried to argue about the sensible value of the wall, they were shouted down. "Those stories are for children. We are grown up. We will demolish the wall." And with great enthusiasm they began to tear down the wall.

Since they began this task in the summertime when the sea was calm, their first view of the beach was a cause of rejoicing. The novelty of their first frolic in the surf sent them back with renewed energies to topple more of the wall. By wintertime enough of the wall was gone so that when the storms began to rage, the great waves flooded in. The lovely homes were battered to pieces, the gardens were inundated. Those fortunate enough to escape with their lives clambered to the treetops and there, clinging for dear life, stared at the roiling waters in fright. Some cried for all that was lost.

No doubt one can view a commitment of fidelity as a prison wall if one so chooses. But from another point of view it may be seen as a protective rampart with proud flags flying, within which a couple know a profound sense of security in their love relationship. Having assured each other with solemn promises that they will not let any threat or temptation breach that wall, they can set about building their abode of love and planting their garden of delights. Precisely because the enhancement of their relationship takes time, they benefit from knowing that, no matter what storms the future may bring, or how high the waves of change in circumstances may crest, they will have the time of their lives. Indeed, without a promise of fidelity, their freedom to build or plant would be drastically curtailed for time would be against them. Sooner or later, one storm or another would destroy their relationship.

To appreciate why this is so, we have only to recognize that marriage is not a static condition, but an ongoing process. It is not a living arrangement, but a lifelong adventure. It is not an adventure of conquest, such as the conquest of Everest or of Peru, but an adventure of discovery: the discovery of one another. Far from requiring that they leave their commitment behind, this adventure depends very much on a couple's appreciation of the permanence of their commitment.

Their discovery of one another involves getting to know one another ever more intimately, yet it is not a mere intellectual journey, no matter how much insight it requires, wisdom it offers, thoughtfulness it takes. Personal intimacy is sought. That means that the total person is involved in the knowing. Not only is that knowing not strictly an intellectual trip, it involves "carnal knowledge." As in the Old Testament the word "yada," meaning "to know," is used for sexual relations, so their knowing of one another involves their bodily experiences of each other.

Precisely because we are persons, we can never in this life be known totally by another. Even in a lifetime we cannot exhaust the capacity of the other to surprise us. That is why marriage is more a lifetime task of "getting to know" one another than it is a matter of actually knowing. It is also true that we cannot usually know another more intimately than the other wishes to be known. The truest knowledge of the other is built up out of the revelations of self the other freely makes to us.

It happens from time to time that we remark of someone: "He gave himself away with that statement." We're referring to a glimpse caught of the inner workings of the man, the person he truly is, whatever the mask he wears before the world shows. Most of us are careful most of the time not to "give ourselves away." We are acutely conscious of the fact that presenting that kind of gift is living dangerously. We aren't very comfortable about letting others know us too well; we sense that such knowledge gives the other a degree of power over us. All of our instincts are for self-preservation. We know how vulnerable we are, how easily hurt we can be. Experience tells us we can be exploited if we aren't careful with our selves.

If I take off my armor, you can hurt me more easily. If I lift my mask, you may reject the face you see. If I give something of myself to you, you may take the gift and run away, leaving me with a sense of depletion, rejection, or betrayal. Or you might use that knowledge of me to manipulate me. This painful awareness of our own vulnerability accounts for our reluctance to lightly "give ourselves away."

At the same time we all yearn to be loved and accepted for ourselves alone. We hunger for community (union with), someone else. We desire to be accepted by another in a way that is not conditioned by what we have or do not have, or by any of the superficial things, the accidentals we share with so many others. We want to share ourselves with someone who accepts us for who we are in our uniqueness. But because of our vulnerability, we seek assurances that ours is not a temporary meeting. We seek some pledge that our total gift of self will be reciprocated by the total gift of the other's self. We want to hear: "You, as you are, actually and potentially, this instant and in the future, are sufficient for me. I accept you unconditionally." The marital vow is that sort of statement, a solemn pledge that we shall have and hold one another, cherish one another, through all the vicissitudes of life, for better or worse, allowing no other to come between us, until death.

Psychologist Sidney Jourard, in his work *The Transparent Self* (New York: D. Van Nostrand, 1964) defines a healthy relationship between two loving people as "characterized by mutual knowledge, openness of communication, freedom to be oneself in the presence of the other without connivance, and respect, to name a few criteria." It is doubtful these characteristics can be fully realized by a couple whose relationship is of its very nature tentative, where they are saying to each other, "I love you now, but I may not love you tomorrow. I want you now, but I don't know about next week. I accept you now, but I might not accept you if you change or grow or displease me."

Jourard comments:

> The optimum in a marriage relationship, as in any relationship between persons, is a relationship between I and Thou, where the partner is being himself in the transaction, without reserve, faking or contrivance, disclosing himself as he is in a spirit of goodwill. The ideal is difficult and rarely achieved. In most relationships, it is experienced as moments of rare meeting, of communion. Certainly such moments, when *she* becomes truly *thou*, are experienced with joy. When she becomes thou, a person, he or she becomes unpredictable, spontaneous, and the other likewise becomes spontaneous. At those times, or when two people are capable of such moments, their sex life will be exquisite. This is almost to say that, given reasonable lack of prudery, a lusty, joyous, and yet holy and sometimes awe-inspiring sex life grows best out of a relationship between two persons who can be themselves with one another without fear of being deeply hurt when they are so unguarded. The very defenses which protect one from being hurt by one's spouse's remarks, deeds, or omissions are the very defenses which impede spontaneous sexuality. Openness before a person renders one open to sights, sounds, smells in the world, and also open to the riches of one's own feelings. The person who effectively guards himself against pain from the outside just as effectively ensures virtual sexual anesthesia.

The commitment of fidelity, each to each, is the heartbeat of a successful, a living marriage. It is the vow which permits the couple utmost freedom to be themselves, allows them to give themselves away, to grow and change and express themselves honestly with one another without fear of rejection. As a result, they are able to know the spontaneous joys of giving and receiving full sexual surrender.

Psychologist/counselor Henri J. M. Nouwen, in his book *Intimacy* (Notre Dame, Ind: Fides Publishers, Inc., 1969), comments:

> When the physical encounter of men and women in the intimate act of intercourse is not an expression of their total availability to each other, the creative fellowship of the weak* is not yet reached. Every sexual relationship with built-in reservations, with mental restrictions or time limits, is still part of the taking structure. It means "I want you now, but not tomorrow. I want something from you, but I don't want you." Love is limitless. Only when men and women give themselves to each other in total surrender, that is with their whole person for their whole life, can their encounter bear full fruits. When through the careful growth of their relationship men and women have come to the freedom of total disarmament, their giving also becomes a for-giving, their nakedness does not evoke shame but desire to share, and their ultimate vulnerability becomes the core of their mutual strength. New life is born in the state of total vulnerability—that is the mystery of love. Power kills. Weakness creates. It creates autonomy, self-awareness and freedom. It creates openness to give and receive in mutuality. And finally it creates the good ground on which new life can come to full maturity and development.

All of the evidence, then, indicates that personal freedom, the richest personal experiences, and the most complete sensual pleasures do not flow out of lack of commitment. Nor is lack of commitment itself to be equated with freedom. In fact, to make a choice, to make a commitment, is one of the ways in which we most fully exercise our freedom. To avoid choices and decisions, to shun commitments is to avoid using our freedom. It is the nature and quality of our commitments—to self and to others—which give direction and meaning to our lives. The person shunning commitments is at the same time abdicating the role of creator of his own life's meaningfulness; he lays himself open to being the victim of every passing fad, the creature

---

*Nouwen's phrase for those who freely "give themselves away" in self-disclosure.

of circumstance, the plaything of external pressures; his life is spent coping with the momentary rather than taking responsibility for creating his own future.

The vow of fidelity is, however, not a mere formula we uttered once upon a time. The quality of that commitment, even at the time we make it, depends heavily upon the degree to which it is not falsified or weakened by inner reservations. There is a sense in which the promises made are renewed throughout the marriage. On the happier side, the experience of the mutual pleasure and joy we share strengthens and reaffirms our unity. On less happy occasions, the times when our unity is threatened by conflict or personal tensions—one partner withdrawing from the other, changing in ways that the other finds uncomfortable or even hurtful—the promise to be faithful meets the very challenges that called it into being. It is here, in crisis, that the mutual pledge demands of us that we take steps to solve the problems, assume responsibility for transcending our immediate desire to withdraw ourselves, and instead seek creative ways of overcoming the difficulties. This may involve our drawing upon resources of spirit and body previously untapped in order that we can see this period of "worse" through. Sometimes, in drastic cases, only our faithfulness to ourselves, our refusal to break our pledge, may sustain us—the other has made himself so inaccessible to us, or is making acceptance of him so difficult. Yet, it is only when such times do come that the commitment shows its necessity at all, that it is put to the task for which it was forged: sustaining our mutuality through periods of drought as well of those of harvest.

The most popularly held misconception about fidelity is that it is defined solely in terms of sexual exclusivity. Many, asked to define the term, would reply simply: "It means you don't commit adultery." Because of this impoverished notion of fidelity, many marriages which are unmarred by sexual activity outside the marital relationship are yet scarred by infidelity within it. The commitment of fidelity to the other goes far beyond such a simplistic definition.

It means that I will first of all be faithful to myself, not pretend or wear a mask before you so that you cannot know me. I will be honest with you. I will open myself out to you as I am, letting you know me and the emotions I feel, the hopes I have, the fears that strike me. Moreover, my commitment in fidelity includes my welcoming your expressions of yourself; meeting you where you are at now; treating you with all the respect owed to a person, with all the tenderness and understanding owed to one who is easily hurt. Fidelity to you means that I will seek to empathize with your feelings, try to look at things from your point of view. I will help in fulfilling the best of your human potential and I will not harden my heart against you, cut you off from me, spiritually divorce you, should your behavior, your attitudes, your wishes, or your words pose a threat to me, fail to coincide with my own, or even cause me pain.

When forgiveness is called for, my faithfulness requires that I be willing to forgive, not with the self-righteous forgiveness of one who thinks himself superior, but with that forgiveness of one who knows his own need to be forgiven by the other. Our reconciliation will not be the abject surrender of one will to another, but the loving embrace of equals who know that, whatever their differences or misunderstandings, they will work them out together.

Our fidelity involves our not "taking one another for granted," but recognizing, and in very real ways affirming, our gratitude at the mystery and the wonder of the other's presence in our lives. Fidelity is expressed in a relationship when each is aware that their relationship has priority over all other matters. The man who puts nearly all of himself into his work and leaves his wife only the leftovers is committing a form of adultery. Many a wife has commented: "He loves his job more than me." The woman who invests her greatest energies in housekeeping, her job, her children, and only gives her husband the remnants of her time and attention has likewise been unfaithful to her commitment. More than one husband, having succumbed to an "affair" because he was starved for the time and attention of his wife, has said: "She's married to the house and kids, not to me." Here one form of infidelity to the primary relationship of the couple has led to another form of infidelity to that same commitment.

My commitment in fidelity to you is diminished to the degree that I begin to condition my acceptance of you, to withhold myself unless you meet certain performance standards, to play roles, to close the doors of myself against you and permit our estrangement to grow. All of these are failures to live up to my commitment. Some of them can take forms much more seriously damaging to both of us than an act of sexual infidelity. For by permitting certain harmful patterns to grow in our relationship, letting estrangement between us solidify into a mere cohabitational arrangement, I'm slamming the doors on all that our relationship has to offer us in the way of our full growth as human beings and our full enjoyment of true intimacy in marriage. In doing so I am being unfaithful to our basic two-in-one relationship.

Because we learn with the passage of time, because our growth—even our growth in love—demands time, we need lifelong intimacy with one another if we are to reach the highest levels of appreciation of one another's uniqueness. Because true joy in sexuality depends upon my ability to give myself totally, unreservedly, to you, our commitment, by its nature, involves sexual exclusivity. For our sexual giving is, at its best, an expression of our gift of ourselves. And when it means that, this felt experience of our unconditional acceptance of and by the other can be an exhilarating delight beyond parallel. It offers its most marvelous pleasures, experiences of unity which "make" love, and are a powerful incentive to greater loving. Yet these indescribable experiences are an outgrowth of a unity already—and sometimes at great cost—won by the couple, a unity predicated upon their appreciation of the faithfulness of one another, the wholehearted and unconditional quality of their mutual commitment.

Most couples are still struggling to reach a point of mutual confidence. Some find their tensions increasing at the very time they had once assumed they would diminish:

middle age. But there are specific tensions in the middle years of marriage which in some marriages threaten the commitment of the couple, especially in the area of sexual fidelity. As Masters and Johnson pointed out, the contemporary climate of opinion has caused many to question the very foundations of their marriages. Today's accepted sexual mores contrast sharply with the attitudes we had when we first offered one another our pledge of fidelity. Add to this general background more specific problems we confront in our middle years—fears of aging in a society that idolizes youth, worry about sexual potency or attractiveness, the common impulse to get more out of life than we have so far, to name a few—and we have factors breeding a spirit of restlessness about our commitment.

Some marriages have lost whatever husband/wife intimacy they had in earlier years and have drifted into a sort of functional and lifeless relationship. Some married couples have the feeling that they "know" one another—their arguments as well as their lovemaking are routine—and they are bored. More, perhaps, feel they are not understood or appreciated by their spouse. The estrangement can be very profound. A wife in an emotionally/psychologically starved condition can dread being touched by her husband. Not being accepted for herself, she is revolted at being used, physically put off at being used.

In the face of such conditions as these in their marriage, some men and women simply set their teeth and cling grimly to the status quo because they don't know what to do or where to go. One such was the wife who confided: "I'd divorce him, but I'm too accustomed to our life style." Others accept the situation as the "will of God," or merely assume that is the way marriage is supposed to be: the lively and lifelong love affair is judged now to be no more than an idealistic dream.

Some try to maintain the marriage, but seek outside gratification of their personal needs. There are many possible reasons for one to be sexually unfaithful to one's spouse: sexual curiosity on the part of those who had little or no sexual experience prior to marriage and now, in the middle years, fear they may have missed something; wanting to punish one's spouse; looking for reassurance about one's sexual attractiveness; consciously or unconsciously wanting to be "found out" by the spouse, thereby dramatically dynamiting a static situation. Yet more often than not, sexual infidelity is but a symptom of a marriage already damaged by those other infidelities we described earlier.

It has been my experience that affairs are often entered into by married men and women less for sexual gratification than because the human need for loving acceptance, respect, understanding are no longer being met by the spouse. Thus, the man who had an affair and later divorced his wife to marry the woman (who was, cruelest cut of all, older than his wife) said: "She makes me feel very special." Married women, speaking of their reasons for involvement with men other than their husbands, have said: "He was interested in me as a person. I was the most important person in the world when I was with him." "He was sensitive to where I was at; he really cared about me." "He encouraged me to be myself, something my husband never did." One woman sustained an affair for over a year with a man who was impotent: "It was so beautiful. We shared on a level impossible between my husband and me at that time."

It is safe to say that sexual infidelity is a rare occurence among those marriages in which the spouses have nurtured true intimacy on all levels. If the husband and wife have received assurances of the other's acceptance, have a high level of self-disclosure, are involved in a wholehearted affirmation of the other and a nurturing of the other's pleasure in life and in himself/herself, that relationship—having kept the pledge of fidelity to the spouse's good—has little motive for sexual infidelity.

The following story was told by a middle-aged married man, somewhat of a celebrity, about himself. While making a personal appearance in a city away from his home, he attended an evening reception in his honor. His hostess, who was not married, took him aside before the evening was over to ask him privately: "Do you have any sort of arrangement with your wife?"

"What about?"

"About sleeping with others."

"Yes, I do. We don't."

"I'm surprised at you. You're such a liberal, open man. I never took you for a prude."

"Sorry, but I love my wife, and I don't think she'd agree with you about my being a prude."

"Well, you really turn me on, and I'd like you to stay with me tonight. It would mean a lot to me."

"It's a flattering invitation, but it really wouldn't mean a lot to me, so you'd be disappointed, I'm sure."

"Oh, it would be great fun, and your wife would never know about it."

"Even if she didn't, I'd know, and that would make me a different person in my relationship with her."

He spoke of the episode in the context of a conversation about current sexual attitudes, and he said: "I couldn't make her understand that for me sex is the gift of self I make to my wife and she to me. Our lovemaking extends back over twenty years of what we are to one another, where we've been with one another, what we've been through together. We've spent our entire marriage getting it together, and this woman expected me to have the same feeling responses to her in a few hours of purely physical fiddling around." He had turned aside an opportunity for sexual infidelity, not for negative reasons but for the positive ones that were so apparent to him. He was one of those for whom sexual infidelity was not so much a matter of right or wrong as a matter of not being necessary.

Those of us who haven't experienced that sort of sexual communion can look at the totality of our relationship and ask ourselves what we can do to enhance our sense of oneness with our spouses. The revivification of our own marriages is not an impossibility. Unfortunately, an individual can put forth enormous amounts of emotional energy on an extramarital relationship, spend creative efforts to make time for it, and yet not see that an equal amount of time and energy devoted to renewing the love affair with the spouse might turn that marriage around. Perhaps it is his not doing such things for and with his wife that has caused their marriage to lose some of its life. And is it not likely that because he is giving his best energies to someone else, their marriage is lately more passionless than ever, has diminished in moments of joy? He complains of her attitude, but isn't his dilution of his personal commitment to her conditioning her responsiveness to him?

Too many of us who vowed to "give ourselves away" to the other have gradually withdrawn that gift of self. We are no longer offering ourselves wholeheartedly and each of us suffers from that shrinking back into our own skins. The longer we permit the situation to endure, the more alienated from each other we become. We might ask ourselves if it isn't our own infidelity to the promise, in ways both small and large, that may be the cause of our boredom or discontent. Rather than trying to overcome our sense of estrangement or loneliness by further infidelity, this time sexual, we might make conscious attempts at enlivening our marriages, at re-creating them.

There are couples who renew their marriage vows regularly, say every fifth anniversary. Most churches have a formal ceremony for this and it makes a beautiful part of the anniversary celebration. The vows, which may not have been clearly heard by the couple caught up in the excitement of their wedding day, gain new meaning in the context of their experiences so far. The renewal of the marriage commitment need not take place in a formal ceremony, however. An individual can simply resolve privately to rededicate himself/herself to the other's well-being.

Such a renewed commitment of the will to the good of the other, followed by creative actions designed to bring pleasure and joy to the other, and by those signs, words, and gestures that nourish the other's sense of well-being and self-esteem, can be the start of a deeper and more gratifying relationship than ever experienced before. The very pains of growing up together this far have taught us much about each other and about life as it is. Unlike the lovers whose high ardor is the result of ignorance—an ardor compounded as much of projected desires and fervent personal needs as of the quality of the other—and whose sufferings as they come to terms with reality are in the future, we have tasted each other, we have felt and smelled each other. We know one another in our nakedness, and we've seen one another respond to sickness, to threat, to pain, to all that life could throw at us in the years we've been together. We are far from ignorant of each other. For us to reaffirm our love at this juncture of our lives, to devote renewed energies to enhancing our relationship, is a much more meaningful gesture of love than our very first exchange of those same words.

The German theologian, Dietrich Bonhoeffer, while imprisoned and awaiting execution by Hitler's Gestapo, wrote a sermon for the wedding of a young couple of his acquaintance. In it he said: "It is not your love which sustains the marriage, but from now on the marriage that sustains your love." Put another way, our early love for each other was heavily laced with strong physical drives and, perhaps, other personal needs that fed our erotic attraction to one another and led to our marriage. In our early years we shared many external things because of that erotic love. As the years passed, however, the balance shifted somewhat so that the quality of our shared life, our shared years, now finds expression in our marital embrace. It is our marriage commitment that sustains our love, even in its erotic dimensions; for the quality of our commitment to one another heavily influences our sexual responsiveness, our physical delight or lack of it. The couple who direct themselves toward enriching their monogamous commitment through a more total sharing of self, who focus their best emotional, sexual, and creative energies exclusively on one another, are those whose lives are open to the truest sexual freedom with one another. Not only will they experience exquisite moments of joy in their sexual giving, but they will see their faithful love create truly liberated spouses who continue to freely and totally reciprocate their loving.

CHAPTER III

CREATIVE
CONFLICT

Marriage is, in the hallowed phrase, "a covenant of intimacy," a relationship of closest physical, emotional, and spiritual contact between two persons. In the early days of our discovery of each other, it was this desire for the deepest possible union of our lives that elicited from us the decision to marry. In the high ardor of those courtship days, impelled by the power of our erotic love for one another, we joyed in merely being together. Our communion, our union-with, each other seemed in itself the only necessity for good communication between us; our understanding and empathy flowed effortlessly.

Each marriage is unique, but few have that experience of effortless unity endure for an extended period of time. To expect it is to suffer from a romantic illusion. The reality of the situation is that we are different persons—sexually, in our family backgrounds, in our personal histories— uniquely ourselves. It was the recognition of that "difference," that "uniqueness," which was part of the attraction we felt toward each other. We ought not wonder, then, that some marriages do not enjoy the sense of effortless unity beyond a few weeks or months, that most do not enjoy it beyond the first year or so of marriage, before those differences between us show themselves in conflict situations.

Even if resolved, some conflicts leave scar tissue tender to the touch for years to come. If unresolved, they become sources of estrangement, so many bricks in a wall separating us each from the other. Even when the estrangement does not lead to divorce, there can be a sort of divorce between us, a sense of alienation from the other, of isolation within the marriage. Such a marriage, to a greater or lesser degree, becomes a "marriage of strangers" where true intimacy does not exist. A sort of functional cohabitational arrangement replaces the former delight in getting to know each other better. Even when this does not degenerate into the sort of bitterness that caused one woman to quote Publius Syrus and say: "I guess it's true that familiarity breeds contempt," it is nonetheless a situation sterile of the pleasure and impoverished of the deep satisfaction that the reality of a living marriage offers us and that is possible for us.

The origins of such estrangement may have nothing to do with our relationship itself, but go back beyond our first encounter with one another. Indeed, the most common barrier to intimacy in marriage has its roots in our childhood and often was firmly established at the very moment of our saying "yes" to the covenant of intimacy that is marriage.

All too many of us suffer from a low level of self-esteem. Our lack of self-love and self-appreciation was seeded into us in our earliest years. There are few parents who did not do their very best for their children; but too many of us in our formative years did not get enough reassurance that we were lovable simply because we were ourselves. Perhaps our parents believed, like their parents, that "children should be seen but not heard," and so we were treated as less than persons. Perhaps, caught up in the depression period's struggle for survival, they simply had little time for us and our concerns. It could be that—in mistaken zeal to have us do well in life—they placed too much emphasis upon school work or other achievements, leading us to believe that their love was conditional upon our accomplishments. Maybe they argued all the time, fought over the way we were to be disciplined, caused us to believe that if we weren't around they would be at peace with one another. It could be that they paid little attention to our personal needs, but thought that their love was shown through material gifts. Some were so determined not to "spoil" us that they were much more demanding than loving. Some, at the other extreme, were so permissive that we got the message that they simply didn't care what we did, which translated rapidly into our conviction that they didn't care for us. Perhaps it was a more severe trauma, a divorce during our childhood or adolescence: "He never really loved me, or he wouldn't have left mother and me." "If I hadn't been such a burden to them, perhaps they wouldn't have divorced."

The list of possible causes is as long as we care to make it. We must not forget that significant adults other than parents may have contributed to our low self-esteem. The teacher scowling with disgust: "You're a cheater," towers over the panicked child. The child, having tried to get a good grade only so his parents would be proud of him, cries, "I didn't cheat." "Now you're a liar," she announces, the judgment burning into him like a brand. Our peers, too, may have furthered our sense of being basically unlovable. "Harry's a sissy, don't play with him." "Go away, Jean, we don't want ugly fatsos in our club." For nearly all of us, it was a number of such experiences which contributed to our feelings that we weren't lovable in ourselves, like other people.

Not aware that most others shared somewhat the same feelings of inadequacy, of inferiority, we kept those feelings to ourselves and tried to behave as if we were just like everybody else—those fortunate others we saw around us who appeared so self-assured, self-confident, adequate to the problems of life. We matured, having learned to keep our deepest feelings hidden, our true selves to ourselves, and having designed for ourselves a *persona*, a public person, which we showed to others.

And one day while pilgrimaging through life, we

bumped into this other person who seemed totally different from anyone else we had ever met, a person unique in our experience. Our whole being flowed out to this other in a spontaneous movement toward union, a desire to be united with the other—which is the basic thrust of erotic love. That ecstasy—which, as well as meaning "outflowing," can be defined as "being beside oneself"—is what caused our friends to say: "He's just crazy about her," or "She's wild about him." The other person had become the center of our thoughts, our concerns, our daily existence. Possibly it was those same friends who, speaking to one another, said: "I don't know what she sees in him," "What on earth does he see in her?" "What do they see in each other?"

What we "saw," of course, was the true uniqueness of this other person as a person, this precious, never to be duplicated, irreplacable, lovable human being. And because we were so intensely centered upon one another, we were capable of saying: "I thought you were going to say that." "I thought you'd call." "I knew it was you on the telephone." And we agree: "We must have ESP." At this point, anyone who told us that we might have communications problems, barriers to intimacy, would be met with total disbelief. '

So, having found each other, the other half of our humanity without whom we knew we'd never feel whole, we heard "I love you. Let's get married." If we suffer from low self-esteem, this declaration has a twofold effect. First it sets off a wild celebrational event in our consciousness, complete with skyrockets, swelling crescendos, and doves rising heavenward. Our whole being shouts "Yes," and we desire nothing more than lifelong union with the other half of our humanity. We want to continue the joy and happiness of discovery for our entire lifetime. Yet, while that celebration is going on, there is something else occurring. Something very like a little computer whirring silently in the hidden recesses of our consciousness, sending out a "tilt" signal and delivering the message: "But this person can't love you. You're not lovable. You don't even love yourself." It must be that the other is able to say "I love you" because they don't know us as we know ourselves.

It is at this juncture that some choose to run from commitment, fearing the other's discovery of their true selves. If we decide to say "Yes," at the same time we firmly resolve, in the hope of preserving the other's love for us, never to let the other know us as we really are. So, at the moment of committing ourselves to the covenant of intimacy, we have slammed a door against true intimacy and think we're protecting our love by this resolve.

Of course, we're not protecting our relationship at all. In fact, we've sown the seed of enormous pain and perhaps the breakup of our marriage. For it is not long after the marriage that the other, still attuned in that keenly attentive way, asks:

"What's wrong, honey?"

They are aware of something hurting us. The hurt is rather like the hurt of the starving man invited to attend a banquet, but only as a spectator; he suffers more severe pangs than when huddled in the cold doorway outside. We have come to a banquet of intimacy, but do not permit ourselves to partake for fear the discovery of our true selves will cost us love. The question, however, is like a hand turning the knob of the door which we have deliberately locked against our spouse; the doorway to ourselves, the self we believe to be unlovable. So we respond by holding the door closed. "Nothing's wrong."

But love is persistent. "Something's wrong. You want to talk about it?"

We must throw more weight against the door to keep the other out. "I said nothing's wrong and I mean nothing's wrong."

"But you're not happy lately."

"Damn it, I'm happy! Just leave me alone, will you!"

Often enough, in such a situation, the bride or groom will talk with friends of the total personality change in the other, how sullen and withdrawn, even belligerently defensive the spouse has become, when before marriage he or she was so considerate, loving, thoughtful, open. Of course, if both are suffering from the lack of a proper self-love, the situation is compounded even more drastically. The couple may end up profoundly ratifying one another's feelings of insecurity or alienation, and confirm for one another their basic sense of being unlovable. Many of our early divorces stem from this very situation, one party fleeing the pain and hurt inflicted by the change in the other's behavior, or both running from a relationship so drastically different from what each had yearned for and dreamed about. Yet the barrier to their joy in intimacy with one another was not raised by events after the wedding, but posited at the very moment of their having said "yes" to the covenant of intimacy.

Most of us are not so severely wounded that we have no self-esteem at all. Some of us, indeed, through the affirmation given by the love the other has for us, can grow in self-appreciation through the marriage relationship to an ever healthier opinion of ourselves. Yet, nearly all of us have fears of our own inadequacies, that painful awareness of our shortcomings that can make true intimacy a fearful venture on our part. These fears, rooted in a sense of our own vulnerability, make it hard for us to communicate ourselves to one another honestly.

That is why, when we do make such attempts and are rebuffed, it is so difficult for us to try again. Certain topics in the course of our marriage may, by unspoken agreement, have become taboo—not raised for fear of suffering again the hurt felt the first time they were brought into the open and ended in an argument that resolved nothing. Should the topic come up, or be alluded to by one partner, the other raises a sternly defensive barrier and shoots it down by quick overreaction or the refusal to discuss it. The disagreement continues under a sort of armed-truce arrangement: as long as it is not brought up, we won't fight. As we shall see in later chapters, sex is often one of those taboo topics, but whatever the list for any couple might include, it is a list of obstacles to true intimacy in the marriage.

Some couples, however, do fight—and regularly—and they always argue about the same things: be they sex, money, raising the children, the in-laws. But the reason they fight so regularly is because their arguments never resolve the matter to their mutual satisfaction. The arguments may be of greater or lesser intensity, but they always follow the same pattern, the same script. When the particular issue is brought up, the couple step into their roles and carry the scene to its habitual conclusion: she bursting into tears and slamming the bathroom door, or he slamming the front door on his own last word. They know the argument so well that if one were to forget a line, the other would be able to supply it. In some marriages the same arguments have had a run of fifteen years or more, with the same results: emotional upset, a period of "silent treatment," a time of licking one's own wounds, and a gradual return to the state of functional normalcy that existed prior to the argument. This may occur with or without a "making up" scene, but the basic issue still remains unresolved.

It might be suggested facetiously that such a couple tape-record these standard arguments. Then, the next time they are going to have the argument on sex, money, or the in-laws, they could pluck the appropriate tape from the shelf, put it in the cassette player, and go out to dinner or a movie. At least, that would save them from the emotional wear and tear of the scene and would provide the same nonresults. There are, of course, more creative ways of handling this and other situations. Before we discuss these in detail, it might be useful to consider the matter of marital conflict situations in a general way.

Many of us fear conflict situations not only for the reasons given above, but also because we have the mistaken notion that expressing negative feelings aroused in us by the other is an unloving act. Indeed, in courtship days we may have had few negative feelings at all toward the other. Actually, when we did see negative qualities, if we were like most romantic lovers, we translated them immediately into positive ones by an alchemy stimulated by our high ardor.

The young husband of two years protests that his wife is impossible to live with. "She's so sloppy, careless, and irresponsible." Later, when led to discuss attractive qualities of the girl prior to their marriage, the same young man speaks of how "carefree and spontaneous" she was. The intimacy of marriage is a daily growing up in an appreciation of the fact that the other is no more perfect than any other human being. However, we may find it difficult indeed to shift gears and bring ourselves to express negative feelings. How to do it without hurting the other? Or perhaps the fear that open conflict would result holds us back. How can love flourish if we're in conflict? Besides, we reason, open confrontation on this issue will be painful and might do more harm than good.

There are marriages of long standing in which the parties have very little dialogue upon the things that matter most to each of them. Fear of conflict, or the hurt feelings that stemmed from previous attempts at discussion may have led to a mutual wariness. Many such couples avoid occasions where they might have to spend extended lengths of time alone together. They quietly collude to avoid such times when they might have to talk about more than the job, the bills, the children. If she suggests: "Let's go out to dinner tonight," he promptly responds with, "Good idea, I'll see if the Staleys want to come along." If he says, "I was thinking we might go to the cabin this weekend," she says, "Oh, great. I'll see if the McBrides can make it." Often, she will analyze her marital relationship with her close women friends, talk of her frustrations, fears, and feelings with more honesty and depth than she is able to with her husband. He, if at all typical of the American male, speaks of these things to almost no one. The two of them are involved in a stale-mate. On the surface, many of their friends might even consider them an ideal couple because they function so smoothly and without any obvious conflict. Underneath, they are a couple terrified of getting involved in anything approaching true intimacy with one another.

Some marriages are kept in the stale-mate situation because one spouse avoids conflict by merely agreeing to or "going along with" everything the other says or wishes to do. This method sometimes becomes the "I know I'm always wrong," the "You know best," or the "Whatever you say" tactic. This is usually the same person who will avoid any conflict by posing his or her desires or feelings as questions rather than statements: "Would you like to go to the movies?" rather than "I feel like going to the movies." Often, the negative response to a desire expressed as a question, even if acceded to, leads to feelings of being unloved and fosters hidden resentments: "She never wants to go to the movies when I do." At the same time it permits shifting the responsibility of decision to the spouse, even so slight a decision as whether or not we go to the movies.

Some avoid expression of feelings and open conflict by being objective, rational, sticking to the facts, and talking theory or abstractions. Expressions of feelings by the other are seen as unimportant; what is important is the factual data. Men seem more guilty of this tactic than women, especially men who are themselves involved in work that is abstract, technical, objective. This method of avoiding empathetic contact with the other is more exasperating than the method of constant agreement, but both are used as barriers to intimacy by the person; and both are deliberate ways of avoiding open dialogue about deep feelings, steering clear of that true intimacy that risks speaking from the center of oneself.

It might be well, in such cases, to approach this sort of situation directly, aggressively: "I don't care what you *think* about it, I want to know what you *feel* about it." "The question is not whether I want to go to the movies, but whether you want to go to the movies."

In both situations, when our response changes from acquiescence in the behavior to a refusal to collaborate in these avoidance moves, the other party is forced into more open dialogue on the matter. It means the deliberate raising of a conflict because the new response places a demand upon the other, but it is the sort of conflict which, persisted in, can lead the other to more open communication.

In these situations, as in others we will have occasion to discuss, we should not expect miracles. It has taken some of us years to learn to behave as we do, and it should not be expected that we can unlearn such behavior overnight. However, it ought to be kept in mind that nearly all our behavior is, in fact, learned and can be unlearned. The person who shies away from self-sharing because "I'm just naturally shy," or the person who excuses an unwillingness to share himself with others on the grounds of being "naturally a loner," has to be confronted with the question of responsibility. "How long did it take you to become so good at being naturally shy?" "You do that naturally-a-loner bit very well, that must require lots of practice." The "naturally this way" plea is nothing more or less than a resistance to change hidden behind a facade of irresponsibility: "I can't help it, it ain't my fault." But spontaneous behavior, as any combat military man knows, is well-learned behavior. And so the attempt to hide behind the "I was born this way" shield ought to be seen for what it is and confronted for what it is: flight from intimacy.

The fact is that ultimately open dialogue is vital to having a living marriage. And in dialogue, conflict is inevitable between two human beings who have totally different personal histories, belong to different sexes, and look at the world from different perspectives. When two human beings marry, they have set the stage for many differences that will have to be resolved as the couple build the "me" and "you" into a "we" that is mutually enriching for both of them. To avoid that effort—and, yes, that pain—is to avoid working toward that intimacy which is the substance of a living marriage and to settle instead for a "marriage of strangers" or a stale-mated lifestyle.

It might be well for us to understand that the pains that come as a result of honest confrontations in our marriage relationship are growing pains. In most cases, the conflict situation, if properly handled, is but another moment of growth in the relationship. Even the divorce crisis—that moment when the conflict situation has proven so painful that one or both believe divorce is the only solution—is, in the majority of such situations, merely the moment of greatest potential growth in the marriage. One or the other or both are demanding change, wanting the relationship brought to a more satisfactory level. To seek out some competent help to steer them through the divorce crisis— as some have done—might put their relationship into an altogether new orbit. Unfortunately, trapped in their un- resolved conflict situation and feeling the pain so intensely, many choose instead to sunder the relationship and flee the scene. Yet, the pain of conflict can be borne by those who do appreciate that these are pains of new birth in the mar- riage, if worked with and gone through rather than fled from.

The analogy might limp a little, but millions of women in recent years have learned that if, instead of deadening the pain of childbirth with anesthesia, instead of dreading it and fighting it, they learn how to work with the pain, how to read its signs, how to use it, they can make their child- birth experiences one of the most joyous and exhilarating moments of life. Something similar is involved in this mat- ter of the pain of conflict: to run from it is to miss out on what joys may lie on the other side. The problem is that so few of us, at any time in our lives, were really taught how to communicate about the things that mattered most to us. Thus, we don't know how to work with the negatives we feel, how to handle the problems that arise, in order to make our conflict situations more creative.

A first step in the direction of more creative handling of conflict situations would be to consider how we've handled them in the past. Very often, the taped-argument situation is the result of one of us beginning the dialogue by saying: "You *always* . . ." or "You *never* . . ." or "Why don't you . . ." or "You ought to . . ." Consider our response when someone figuratively or literally points a finger and says "You never talk to me anymore." Or, imagine the spontaneous reaction to: "You ought to get that damned door fixed." The words are like an arrow sent into the tender ego. Wounded, the immediate reaction normally is to counterattack: "What do you mean? I'm talking to you right now, aren't I? I talked to you yesterday. What's wrong with *you?*" Or: "When have I had time to get that damned door fixed? I've been going day and night for six weeks on this new deal. Why the hell can't you fix it? You're not helpless." And from there the argument moves along, attack-/counterattack, often leaving both opponents exhausted.

Perhaps the basic rule for improving marital communications is that we should try to avoid all openings that start with "You . . ." and especially those that have "always," "never," "should" or "ought" as their second word. In the first place, such generalizations are seldom accurate. In the second place, they almost demand a counterattack, which leads to a fruitless dialogue.

Often enough we involve ourselves in expressions of anger or resentment toward those around us when it is ourselves we are angry with or resentful about. If, instead, we seek to come to terms with ourselves, to find what part of us is being pinched, frustrated, hurting, and share these feelings, we will have made a move conducive to our own growth and the improvement of our relationship with our spouse. Letting our spouse know of our ambivalent feelings, our felt tensions, is a way of opening ourselves up and also opening some doorways to the other's being able to understand, to cope, and to offer us the supportive love we seek. Our inner conflict has not found outlet in merely destructive outbursts, but has become creative of increased intimacy.

Even when the source of our pain seems to be the other or the other's recent behavior, we ought to reflect upon what is really going on inside of ourselves. Getting in touch with ourselves first will better enable us to handle the situation creatively. Reflection upon our personal feelings may lead us to see that when I was tempted to say "You never talk to me anymore," what I truly felt was "cut off from you." Now, if I accept responsibility for my feelings and try to express them accurately, an altogether different situation might transpire.

"Honey, I'm feeling cut off from you lately." Not only is this statement nonthreatening, nonchallenging, it is an honest attempt to express personal feelings. No one can call it a lie, for only the person involved knows what he or she is feeling. Having exposed my feelings—made a truly intimate comment about myself—the possibilities for the other's responses are manifold.

"I didn't know you felt that way. What's the trouble?" "I know, darling, I've been so damned busy we've not had much time to talk lately." It is possible, of course, in certain marriages, that the other could respond with: "I don't give a damn how you feel," "That's your problem," or even play down the feelings with "That's ridiculous."

If that is the response, then it is necessary to return again to one's feelings and to speak only for ourselves. "I feel like you've just slammed the door on me and I don't know why." The important thing is that by keeping to "I" language and by keeping to the attempt to translate our own feelings into words, the possibility for honest communication and truly intimate exchange is greatly enhanced. Even if the other's response is as drastically negative as that illustration, at least you now know where you stand. More often than not, however, the other's response is less than negative, because by sticking to "I" language and personal feelings, a door has been opened and a red carpet rolled out to welcome the other on that truly intimate level.

In any attempt to improve our mutual dialogue, it is good to keep in mind the value of feedback. That is, prior to responding to the other's remarks, we do well to try to re-express our understanding of what the other has just said. "My sense of what you are saying is . . ." "I feel that you're trying to tell me that . . ." Such feedback has the advantage of insuring that we truly listen empathetically to our spouse in order that we might offer the other our un-derstanding of the statement. The other then has an opportunity to correct us if we've heard wrong or don't yet understand, and our own response comes as an authentic response to what was truly said and understood.

Sometimes, the tape-recorded argument can be avoided and a more creative exchange brought about by the simple expedient of providing such feedback instead of counterattacking, even when the other has begun with a "You . . ." challenge. "You always leave the front room a mess," can be responded to with: "It sounds as if you feel I don't appreciate your housework." Or: "Why don't you fix that damned door?' might be answered: "I think it's not the door you're upset about so much as something else. Want to talk about it?"

Though the other has begun with an attack, this feedback response has broken the phonograph record. The other, having received an unexpected sign of empathy, is called upon to respond in a new fashion. An invitation to intimate dialogue has been offered. An occasion that formerly saw only a waste of emotional energies has now been diverted into an opportunity for true dialogue.

Coming in touch with our true feelings is easier for some than for others. Generally speaking, American men have more difficulty in this area than women. From the time they were told that "Big boys don't cry," through the competitive sports scene into the competitive business scene, they've been educated to the thought that showing fear, tenderness, pain, is "unmanly." We will have more to say on this when we treat of wifely lovemaking. At this point, it is sufficient merely to indicate that, though it might be easier for the generality of women to come in touch with their feelings, it is for all of us, men or women, a crucial factor in any steps toward bettering our communications For, prior to giving honest expression to where we are at, what we need, what we are asking for, we must know these things first ourselves. If too many husbands and wives say things they don't mean, do things they don't understand— and feel miserable for having said and done them—it is because they haven't taken time to engage in the necessary process of self-discovery, have not sorted out the origins of their behavior, but have permitted those feelings to erupt in angry outbursts or damaging behavior directed to the nearest target: usually the spouse.

Part of our problem in communicating ourselves is that we do not like to own up to, to be responsible for, our bad feelings. The term itself carries a moral overtone and we think we "ought not" to feel that way. We judge ourselves harshly for having such feelings, thereby adding to our misery. But moral judgments are out of place in regard to feelings. If we feel this way, that is a fact—we feel this way. If we feel angry about something that happened today, and then tell ourselves that we shouldn't on the grounds that anger is a bad thing, we end up trying to suppress our anger. That usually results in our deflecting it, expressing it in other ways—being moody, irritable, sharp-tongued. Accepting our feelings of anger and saying so—"I feel angry because . . ."—is but one of the more creative options open to us. It also opens the door to our spouse's being able to deal directly with our feelings of anger.

Even if the immediate source of our feelings is the other, it is crucial not to blame the other for our feelings; they are, after all, ours. Not only does "You make me angry . . ." set the stage for the sort of nonproductive dialogue mentioned earlier, it is also factually wrong. The temptation to blame the other is rooted in our desire to pin responsibility for our feelings—especially when we adjudge them bad—upon someone else. If we succeed, the other will feel more guilty than we do about our bad feelings, and we've gained some temporary control over the other through emotional blackmail. But ultimately, such success is no success at all.

Whatever we feel at a given time, we still have the power of choice regarding our response to those feelings. Our chosen response, not the outside situation, event, or person, is the crucial factor in whether we will deal creatively or destructively with regard to ourselves and others. To illustrate this, consider for a moment the ode Robert Herrick wrote "To Daffodils," which most of us read in high school. How many daffodils have we seen in our lifetime and what was our felt response? Perhaps we were content with exclaiming that they were beautiful. Robert Herrick, looking upon the same flowers, had an emotional response which he chose to express in a poem that will live as long as poetry is read. Obviously, daffodils in themselves don't have the power to prompt that response or we'd all have written dozens of odes to them. Rather, the response to the feelings we have depends upon our ability to get in touch with ourselves, to sort out our feelings, and then to look at the options open to us for the creative expression of those feelings.

Many of us hide our true feelings not only from others, even those closest to us, but also from ourselves. Those of us who do this become victims of our moods, creatures of our emotional states, rather than masters of them. Yet any increase in our sense of well-being depends upon our coming to terms with ourselves first of all. Having done so, we are then more able to open ourselves out to others, and especially to share ourselves intimately with that other to whom we are married. The fear of risking this latter step is what has turned many marriages from the path of a lifetime adventure in discovering each other, knowing one another better, loving one another more, into a routinized, almost formalized existence. The yearning for "life" on the part of both may then lead to the filling of the vacuum with social and civic activities, the pursuit of attention through hypochondria, the lapse into alcoholism, or an extramarital affair. Yet, the life yearned for is not found in such remedies, which are mere symptoms of the malady; it is found in devoting time and energies to enhancing the intimate relationship to which the couple have already committed themselves.

Couples trapped in such relationships very often have never really discussed with one another the quality of their union or talked with one another about their current feelings. This mutual silence is partly due to fear; they dread the discovery that they may have nothing in common, or that such a mutual discussion will lead to separation or divorce. Yet a marriage counselor, who uses some Gestalt techniques, recently discussed with me one of his exercises. Seating the husband and wife opposite each other, he asks the wife to say all the bad things she can about her spouse, encouraging her to make the list as long as she can. Then her husband is asked to give a similar list of all his complaints against his wife and to be as exhaustive in his listing as possible. Then the wife is asked to tell of all the good qualities of her husband and he, in his turn, to list all of her good qualities. The therapist commented: "It never fails that they each discover that their negative list is negligible in comparison with their positive list. Often it is the first time that each has learned what the other really appreciates about him or her." While this exercise is not recommended for home use—it definitely requires a qualified facilitator—it serves to illustrate how much some spouses do hide from one another and what discoveries they might make were they to open the doors to honest dialogue.

It is crucial in any dialoguing that we not be seeking to determine who is "right" and who is "wrong." Besides the fact that, given our different perspectives on the reality under discussion we may find this an impossible task, it is simply not fruitful. We are not seeking victories or judgments, but trying to come closer to one another, to make our marriage more alive and enjoyable for each of us.

It may be useful, too, to remind ourselves that "Yes, but . . ." means "No." Also, obviously, calling names, using sarcasm, and making accusations are barriers to good communications between any persons, let alone between spouses. Remembering that we can't read the other's mind or feelings, we can make our remarks exploratory and tentative rather than definitive judgments: "I get the impression this doesn't concern you very much," rather than: "You never give a damn about anything."

Staying in the here and now and remaining specific helps us avoid the debacle of trying to deal with ancient history and of opening old wounds as well as inflicting new ones.

Thus: "You drove Jimmy out of the home with your heavy-handedness and now you're doing it with Donald," is opening the door to a full scale counterattack. Whereas: "I was disappointed in the way you handled Donald's request for the car tonight," may lead to a more productive dialogue.

Timing is a vital factor in communications. Our reactions, our feelings, should be shared as soon as is appropriate so that the other is fully aware of what is being talked about. Storing up hurts or problems and having them overflow all at once at some final provocation is a sure way to waste emotional energy. Some marriages are destroyed, in fact, by one spouse having stored up so many negative feelings that all positive ones are gone. Then when the dumping of stored-up feelings occurs, the other is not only unable to cope with them all at once, the collector of the negative feelings has no desire to try to cope any longer. The discharge of feelings was the parting blast.

Such minimal clues to improving the quality of our verbal dialogue in order to increase our sense of intimacy with each other are basic, but all too often they are not known to couples. Perhaps the most useful single volume containing insights and technical aids to communication is *The Intimate Enemy: How to Fight Fair in Love and Marriage* by Dr George R. Bach and Peter Wyden (New York: Avon Books, 1970). It is a compendium of information on the topic. No couple needs everything in it, but almost any couple will find something to help in their resolution of the conflicts in their relationships.

In seeking means to better our communications with each other, to render our conflicts creative, we must keep in mind that our openness is not an end in itself; it is but the means to enriching our marital life. The risks we are taking—and being open about our feelings, about our sense of where our relationship is at, involves risks—must be understood by both of us to be risks taken for the sake of our mutual relationship. The spouse who understands that this honesty, this expression of feeling, this sharing of oneself, is prompted by the desire to enrich the marriage is, by that knowledge alone, going to be less defensive, more open. We do not take risks of opening ourselves up, of having others become angry with us, of being rebuffed for someone we don't care about. It is precisely because our marriage is so important to us, because this other person is so important to us, that we risk ourselves.

It is necessary to remind ourselves that though any given discussion may be painful in one way or another, it is not aimed so much at getting the partner to change, but at our mutually coming to a better understanding of how we're affecting one another, where we're at with one another, how we view our present situation from our differing perspectives.

Having a relationship of true intimacy means being able to be separate. The worst myth of marriage—one current at a time when many marriages now in their middle years were first entered into—was the "togetherness" myth. It fostered the notion that intimacy demanded our doing all things together, thinking alike, sharing in one another's interests. It was a myth that fostered much unhappiness, causing some to see their differences of opinion as areas of "incompatibility;" others to feel guilty because they had separate interests in certain areas; some to subvert their own interests in favor of their spouse's and to feel unfree, even suffocated, in the relationship.

The truth is that we are not alike and can't expect to be, and that the differences between us are not something to be ashamed of but are the sources whereby we each enrich the other; the sexual difference being but a most obvious example. It is out of the silence of our private moments that we are able to speak most meaningfully to each other. We ought to be striving, in our marital dialogue, to be close, to share on a most intimate level; but also we ought to be respectful of one another's freedom as a person, respectful of the differences between us.

A conflict between us is a creative encounter if it has provided each of us with insight, information, and some degree of a shared understanding of our relationship. Because it is noncoercive, nondemanding, nonjudgmental, each is left free to exercise his or her own options about the future. Since those options will be chosen now with a better understanding of the other's feelings and thoughts, the chances for change are there; but the modification of behavior, the responses, will be freely chosen by each of us.

Those who have been trapped within themselves, playing roles, falling into routines, even those who talk or argue a lot but never really give themselves away, can find anew that the people they married are unique human beings; are people who are constantly growing, constantly changing; are people whose ultimate mystery can never be exhausted; are people who can never be fully known no matter how intimate they become.

That is the truth about all of us. And that is why our marriages can be, if we take responsibility for their quality, a lifetime's delight in discovering one another anew, not only in the joyful things we might do together but in the growing pains, the conflict situations, which all of us sooner or later come to experience; and which we can, if we choose, make more truly creative.

CHAPTER IV

WIFE-WOOING

The mother of five, who just divorced in order to marry another man, says: "I got tired of having six children. He was just the oldest boy in the family. I thought he was a man when I married him. Maybe he was, but as the years went by, he somehow stood still while I continued to grow."

No matter how the particular script reads, the scenario is often the same: a wife making new demands for growth in their relationship; the husband failing to meet those needs.

"Courting a wife takes tenfold the strength of winning an ignorant girl." So wrote John Updike in his gem of a story, "Wife-wooing." Perhaps the reason is rooted precisely in the ignorance of the girl and the lack of such ignorance on the part of one's wife. The "ignorant girl" may be taken in by our struck poses, her fascination with all the unknowns we represent, even by the novelty of our being interested in her at all. For the wife, however, we are someone with whom she has shared years; years marked by times of laughter and days of sorrow; years that have had their bitter words as well as their sweet pleasures; years in which we have seen one another not only physically naked, but emotionally and spiritually so.

By the time we have been married fifteen years or more —if ours has been a relatively normal experience of marriage—we may have succumbed to the notion that we "know" one another so well that the other can offer us few surprises. Indeed, much of our life together, including the fullest physical expression of our relationship, may have become almost routine. A certain plateauing out of the relationship may have occurred. For some, in truth, that plateau may be a veritable desert, without life as far as sexual lovemaking is concerned.

In one study made within the last five years by Duke University's Medical Center, it was revealed that forty-four percent of married women between the ages of forty-five and sixty-five no longer engaged in sexual relations at all. The couples involved in the study agreed that, in most cases, it was the husband's lack of desire to engage in coitus that was responsible. Often enough, when the couple do engage in sexual intercourse, one or both may find the experience less than gratifying. Recently, after one of my lectures, a middle-aged couple invited me to coffee that they might talk privately. They were both physically attractive persons, well educated and articulate.

"In the matter of sexual lovemaking," he said, "I'm in the minor leagues."

I asked him what he meant by that remark.

He said, "Oh, I don't mean she's unhappy about my performance." (To which she promptly added, "Quite the contrary.") "But I get very little personal enjoyment out of it at all. I can take it or leave it and, if it weren't for her, I'd probably not bother."

In many ways, this couple typify a problem not uncommon in marriages in their middle years. They have a stable relationship. They know they love one another. They share the same interests in many areas—working together on various church projects, for example—but they also respect one another's individuality as persons. Unlike the majority mentioned in the last chapter, however, this couple enjoyed open dialogue with each other about their most intimate feelings, even as they were unafraid to bring up for my consideration this matter that was troubling the husband. His experience was, however, not unique, as the survey I cited indicates. Many men in their middle years experience a gradual loss of interest in sexual activity.

It is ironic that this decline of interest and even cessation of sexual lovemaking on the part of many middle-aged husbands should coincide with what amounts to a resurgence of sexual interest on the part of their wives at this very same time. Many women, for whom menopause has meant the end of the fear of pregnancy, experience a sense of sexual freedom unparalleled in their past. Ironic it may be, and yet, perhaps the two factors are related. Prior to discussing the ways in which men may bring new life to their sexual union with their wives, it is necessary to take a look at some of the social conditioning and the attitudes we men share which militate against our own growth in love and decrease our joy in sexual lovemaking.

We American males have grown up with a success mystique in which "success" in a man is measured by his earning power. In today's industrialized and ruthlessly conglomeratized world, where competition is the organizing principle of the system, we learn early in our lives to compete: first in the classroom and on the athletic field, later in the business and professional world. The qualities demanded of us to be successful competitors include aggressiveness, the subordination of our own personal feelings to the goal to be accomplished, manipulative behavior toward others (whether a prospective buyer, an employee, or a superior) and, oftentimes, even a certain ruthlessness toward others. We must appear to be strong, self-assured, in control of the situation. To be successful competitors, we must be on guard lest anyone discover our flaws, for then they could manipulate us through our weaknesses. If our primary goal in life is to be a success in our work, and that success is measured in money, then our primary energies must be expended in that direction. This we call being ambitious about getting ahead.

The man ambitious for success often subordinates relationships, including his spousal relationship, to that goal. Often, too, the very qualities he must permit to flourish in order to be a financial success do not easily coexist alongside those other qualities required to enhance and nurture a love relationship: tenderness, caring, compassion, empathy, openness about himself, willingness to risk being seen as vulnerable.

Perhaps in no other area has the "failure of success" been so manifest, or so well documented, as in the husband/wife relationship. One study (Jan E. Dizard, *Social Change in the Family;* Chicago; Community and Family Study Center, University of Chicago, 1968) followed 400 married couples from the time of their engagement through thirteen to seventeen years of marriage. From expressions of mutual happiness, high levels of cooperation and sharing, and a marked affection for each other revealed in the earlier questionnaire, many couples had moved, by the final questionnaire, to indicating an erosion of their happiness with each other. Half the wives and nearly half the husbands expressed a decline in happiness together. About sixty percent revealed disagreements that were more frequent and serious than those in earlier years. Forty percent of the wives and nearly forty percent of the husbands had considered divorce or separation. Demonstrations of affection had diminished for many.

In an essay based on his study, Dizard commented: "Had all the couples reported declining satisfactions with and commitment to their marriages, we could simply say that time takes its toll. No such bromide applies. In fact what we discovered was that *by and large it was in those couples in which the husband had been most successful in his occupational pursuits that spouses were most likely to report deterioration in the marital relationship.*" (Jan E. Dizard, "The Price of Success," in *The Future of the Family*, edited by Louis K. Howe. New York: Simon and Schuster, 1972. Italics are Mr. Dizard's.)

Indeed, the dissatisfaction and the declining levels of happiness for the most successful husbands and their wives was twice as high as that expressed by those couples whose incomes had actually declined, who were, in short, less successful. Dizard, in the same essay, quotes another study, that of Blood and Wolfe, who reported on nine hundred Detroit-area families: "High income husbands . . . have conspicuously dissatisfied wives."

Tied in with the success mystique that plays so large a part in male attitudes in America, is the performance mentality. From parent/child situations in which love was seemingly given or withheld because of behavior, through schooling situations in which good performance is valued, and the athletic field where it is prized, into job situations where again, good performance is the key to success, the American male is performance- or achievement-oriented. And this performance consciousness has a carryover effect upon the male's approach to sexual activity. All too often, here too, he feels that he is being tested, must perform well sexually.

But how does one measure performance or determine success in the sexual realm? How, indeed? Individual responses to that on the part of men account for the fact that some must "score" (significant word in this context!) with as many women as possible, while others believe that the number of times they can engage in intercourse on the same evening matters; still others may believe that they have failed on any occasion in which their wife has not demonstrated a rapturous orgasmic response. This latter sort of achievement-tripping, in itself, can prove corrosive. One woman, obtaining a divorce after twelve years of marriage, mentioned to me that she had never had an orgasm in the entire twelve years. Her husband was a brilliant man, a high achiever in his field, and very much in love with her. I asked her why, once it had become apparent that she was anorgasmic, she had not sought treatment. "Surely your husband would have cooperated in that," I said.

"Oh, he doesn't know," she replied. "I've been faking it for twelve years."

"But what motivated you to fake orgasm?"

"Well, on our honeymoon, I discovered that he felt such a failure if I didn't come. He was so unhappy that I faked it. He was like a first-grade kid who had gotten a gold star

on his paper, so pleased with himself. And once I began
faking it, how could I stop, or how could I tell him I had
this problem?"

The desire to perform well, however the individual man
measures it, leads the American male into the mechanics-
manual approach to sexual relations. Reared in a technological society, he has been imbued with the spirit of the
technologist who sees the created world as so much
material that can be manipulated to our own comfort and
gratification. Problem-solving characterizes this approach
to the world: every problem can be solved, if only we break
it down into its components and do the right things.

This is a view of the world which has brought immense
blessings to humankind—from transistors aiding the deaf
to hear to satellites charting the heavens—but it is a harmful view when applied to human relations, especially that
most intimate sexual relationship that is marriage. The
anxiety to perform well can, and often does, lead the man
to turn to manuals detailing the mechanics of sexual intercourse, manuals which break the "problem" down into its
component parts—foreplay, lubrication of parts, position-
ing of bodies, climax, postlude—furthering the impression
on his part that if only he can *do* the right things, he will
bring her to orgasm and win his gold star.

This is not an attempt to dissuade anyone from inform-
ing himself about human sexuality. Sexual dysfunction,
marital misery, can come about as the result of sexual ignorance. Some otherwise educated and mature people continue to accept fallacies for fact in sexual matters. Marriages
abound that would benefit enormously from accurate information, supplanting the false assumptions, myths, and
misinformation which presently cripple the couples.

Still, all too many manuals give men the impression that
the expression of our sexual love is a technical performance
and its success depends upon our doing various things or
going through various sexual gymnastics. Not long ago,
two wives were chatting with me during a break in a semi-
nar I was giving and one said: "I wish to hell he had never

read that sex manual. I can mentally hear him turning from page thirty-five to thirty-six and telling himself, 'Now I turn to the left nipple.' "

The other chimed in: "It's worse with me. I can hear my husband mentally licking his thumb to turn the page."

What they were complaining about was that their husbands were so preoccupied with "doing" that they weren't really present for them. The wives sensed that they were mere objects of their husband's manipulation and that the husbands were not even creative in that but following someone else's script.

I've mentioned the "success mystique," the "performance mentality" and the "technological approach" because, in my experience, these are the most common bases from which wifely discontent about husbandly lovemaking arises. They also are often causes of the husband's own dissatisfaction with his marital lovemaking.

To return to the example of the businessman who spoke of his own lack of pleasure in the sexual act. He and his wife have a higher level of intimacy than most marriages, yet he was finding less and less personal enjoyment in lovemaking. Why? Perhaps a clue can be found in his own words. He spoke of himself as being "in the minor leagues" in that area. He said that "she's not unhappy with my performance." The hint of athleticism in the first statement, the outright reference to performance in the second, were the things which I picked up on to discuss with him. I was not surprised to discover that he did approach his sexual relations with his wife as a sort of endurance test and a test of skill, and that "success" was determined by her orgasm. Her only complaint was that he didn't seem to get much out of it and that worried her, but, she added: "Of course, he has an orgasm."

"Does he?" I asked, "Or don't you mean that he ejaculates?"

"Is there a difference?" they both asked, almost in unison.

"You said yourself," I reminded the husband, "that you

got very little personal enjoyment from the act. Does that sound like an orgasm to you?"

"But I do ejaculate."

"Yes, you do. And you may as well be blowing your nose or sneezing, for all the pleasure it brings you. Ejaculation is a physical response. Orgasm is an emotional, psychical response. The levels of orgasmic response in men are just about as variable as they are for women. But because men ejaculate and women do not, and because orgasm occurs normally at ejaculation, many men and nearly all women believe they are the same thing. But if you aren't having an emotional response, aren't getting any psychic pleasure during ejaculation, you aren't having an orgasm."

Clearly evident in this man's situation was something else not uncommon and, in my experience, a source of resentment on the part of some wives: his lack of physical desire for his wife, his lack of physical passion toward her. By his own admission, he was able to "take it or leave it;" he was having sexual intercourse only to please her.

Whether because such men pour their greatest energies into their work, or because they are so concerned with performance that each act of physical lovemaking becomes another trying adequacy test for them, many men seem to approach their sexual activities with their wives in a fashion that is a turn-off for the wife. "If you want to . . ." Or: "We haven't made love in a week, so what about tonight?" There is no hint in this sort of approach that it is the wife's desirability as this particular, unique woman that has prompted the advance. By such infelicitous approaches, some men give their wives the impression that any woman might do; the wife is merely the handy one. Like the "manipulative" approach, this makes them feel they are mere objects. As one woman said bitterly: "I feel like a receptacle for his pent-up sperm." Though that wasn't the case with regard to the couple quoted above, his lack of physical passion is something he shares with these others. He's doing it for her sake. Others are doing it not out of passionate feeling for their wives but out of felt need on their own part—or they are not doing it at all.

This lack of passion in regard to their sexual lives is usually at one with a noticeable lack of passion in regard to life in general. Much of the antimasculine resentment heard from women these days seems related to this growing awareness on their part that many men, including their own husbands, are lifeless, lacking in the passionate caring for the world that these women feel. This situation is heightened in middle age when, according to psychologists, the general tendency is for men after forty to become less aggressive, more pliable; while it is at about this age that women begin to become more self-assertive, more demanding, and often—as pointed out earlier—more sexually alive. The advent of the consciousness-raising efforts of the feminine liberation movement—at its best—underscores women's own feelings, provides a vocabulary for the expression of those feelings, and has helped to legitimatize (if that was needed) their open expression. As a result, many men in their middle years find new demands for change made upon them and are frightened of those demands. Some husbands seek to avoid change or growth by blaming "that fem lib stuff" for their wives' discontent. This is no response to their wives' needs at all. Nor does such labeling make the needs go away. The women's movement only helped wives more openly articulate to their husbands what they were and are feeling. That wives are more openly talking of their emotional and sexual needs is blamed by one psychologist for the alleged increase of impotent men. That is arguable. What is not arguable is that some men are actually frightened by the woman they've lived with for so long; she's changed. If a man feels hostile toward the change, yes, impotency is one way of expressing hostility; so is flight from sexual intercourse.

One wife, whose husband had for years complained of her lack of interest in sex, set to work on her problems in a woman's group therapy situation. She began to take an interest in sexual lovemaking, to show some of the initiative her husband had for so long said he wanted. Her husband reacted by taking one step backward for each step she took forward. Now she finds her own interest waning again.

But flight from lovemaking may also be rooted in the fear that this mature woman, now expressing her personhood in new ways and, perhaps for the first time, making known her own desires in the matter of sexual activity, has lifted the "performance standards" higher than he dares attempt, for fear of proving inadequate. John Updike's line takes on new meaning for such a man—he doubts he has that "tenfold strength."

There is no magic formula for overcoming such problems. But the man who desires to improve his love relationship with his wife does well to examine his own ideas about what constitutes his manhood and how he views sexual intercourse. In one area, where massive layoffs of engineers occured as a result of defense contract cut-backs, therapists were swamped with men who, suffering their first experience of unemployment in their lives, had become impotent. The loss of a job, financial failure, had literally unmanned them. These were men who had defined their masculinity and their success as men in terms of their work, rather than in terms of their persons and their relationship with their wives.

Taking a hard look at ourselves and our own attitudes is but the beginning, however. A second step toward enhancing our enjoyment in our marital relationship is to listen empathetically to what our wives are trying to tell us. In all of my discussions with women on this topic—and I sought out many for input for this chapter—I found the same refrain repeated with regard to marital lovemaking.

Even when I specifically requested insights for use in this chapter meant to center around wife-wooing and sexual lovemaking, no woman was able to isolate that activity from the totality of the husband/wife relationship. What almost all of them talked about was that the man "be a man," "alive," "willing to take initiatives," "be a leader," "one willing to give his life to a cause." One woman said: "You've got these forty-year-old men who really are whiners about their work, about life in general, about their problems. They've got no passion for anything. They only seem to get emotional while watching a football game. And these men are married to forty-year-old women who are, it seems to me especially now, waking up. They're probably more involved, more passionately alive, than they've ever been; and they're just totally turned off by these sexless men. A woman can't be passionately involved unless there's interplay, interaction, because it's not *just* a thing of the body; it's only *partly* a thing of the body. It's very much, with women, a mental turn-on. And so many of these men are turning off women. There's a reason Erica Jong in *Fear of Flying* talks of the woman's search for the man she can share everything with, her search for the 'impossible man —a perfect man whose mind and body are equally fuck- able.' They're looking for him because they don't have anyone like that in their lives."

"Real vitality as a person." "Passionately life-affirming." "One whose motor is going and has energy for everything he's interested in, and everyone." These were other de- scriptive phrases used by women, phrases that flowed into their talk of sexual lovemaking. Indeed, for most, such descriptions seemed to end the discussion for them; such a man they felt they could love, and they were sure he would know how to love them. Pressed further, the next most common word used to describe the husbandly lover was "caring." All were insistent that it was not sufficient that he merely say he cares, but that he show it. "And paying the bills, even providing luxuries," one woman added, "is not sufficient. Today most women can do that for themselves if they need to."

The husband who complained, "I don't know what more she can want from me, she's got a blank checkbook and can buy anything under the sun," was one who felt that his material success had established his credentials as a man and that his "caring" was shown by a blank checkbook. But the Victorian era, when a man could feel that he was a good husband simply because he was a "good provider," is far behind us. The caring these women talked about was that demonstrated concern for their marital relationship, the willingness to put time and energies into that relationship. As one woman put it: "I want my husband to place as much importance upon our relationship as I do, to be as emotionally involved in our marriage as I am."

Another woman, married seventeen years, wrote me: "First I'll tell you what I don't want. I don't want a box of his favorite candy. I don't want to go to the ball game on our 'night out,' and I don't want him (with a martyr's sigh) to begrudgingly take me where I want to go. I don't want a bitchy husband who, on reaching the bedroom, suddenly reverses field and says: 'You look nice, let's fuck.' I don't want to have to say, 'Please, let me tell you about my day.' I don't want to have to tell him it's my birthday, or to ask him to please take the kids to the store as they want to buy me a gift. I don't want threats; I don't to hear: 'You talked to Joe for fifteen minutes at the party!' or 'Boy, did Helen ever notice that you spent most of the evening talking to Bill!' Or again, in the bedroom: 'But you're a nice person, what say we. . . .' I don't want a man in my pocket, looking through the odds and ends of my life. I don't want his demanding all the details of myself as if he has inalienable rights over my inner person. I don't want my worth to be measured by my shape or the action of my behind.

"What do I want? I want to be treated not as a property right but as a human being. I want to be treated as a friend one loves but doesn't always have totally available. I want to be touched—not just in the erogenous zones, but all over my body, my mind, my spirit. I want him to communicate through that kind of touching. I want gentleness, I want real lovemaking. I want him to know that foreplay is something that starts that morning or even the day before. I want him to understand that when he says 'Let's. . . .' his foreplay has occurred in his own mind and he's way ahead of me. That means I have to catch up and, I suppose, if I achieve an orgasm in the interaction, then I'm lucky. I resent that situation and want him to approach it another way. Call it preparation, call it seduction or wooing; but most sex takes place between the ears and I would like to have him see to it that I was 'ready' before I reached the bedroom. I'd like to have no orgasm or one, or two and have no worries about that. I'd like to be able to say, when he's done, 'Now I want even more,' and have that wish fulfilled, too. And, in the end, rather than be able to say good-bye, I'd like to know that we shared a lot of nice hellos —a lifetime of lovely meetings."

What all these women seem to be saying is that the sexual act is not a little island separated from the continent of the couple's daily life, nor is it something one person *does* to another, but rather that the sexual act is an expression of who they are to each other, where they are at with each other, what they mean to each other.

The man trying to prove something to himself in bed, seeking to ring the orgasmic bell so that he can win another medal reading "Man," has already announced that he isn't sure of his manliness. The man who is so intent on performance, so anxious to be given a good grade that his own pleasure is minimal, has likewise revealed his insecurities. The man whose signs of affection and remarks of appreciation for his wife are only given when sexual intercourse is wanted has signaled to her that she is being "used" in the sexual act, rather than loved. He has deprived himself of knowing the fullness of her gift of herself as an expression of love reciprocated.

For the physiological act of sexual intercourse, a penis entering a vagina, is really meaningless in itself. It carries no particular messages on its own, has no specific quality, no particular character, no special significance, no distinctive emotional or spiritual or moral quality. This very same physiological/biological act can be, at one end of the spectrum, the most spiritually enriching, emotionally stirring, physically pleasurable gesture of human love and commitment. At the other end of the spectrum, the very same physical act is second only to murder on the list of indignities one human being can perpetrate upon another—when it is rape.

The act itself has no significance or meaning on its own; that value, that character, that quality, that content is given to it by the two persons involved. And between the two poles mentioned—the ultimate sign of a union in love, and an act of hatred—there are uncountable meanings and nuances possible. These are as varied as the moods of the persons involved. For the same couple, in the space of days, the act may be a tearful act of reconciliation after a quarrel, it may be as celebrational as wedding bells or as tender and subdued as a pavane, it may be as boisterous and noisy as a circus band. But whatever its quality, it speaks of where our relationship is at for that moment, of who we are and what we mean to one another—now.

Many glibly talk of "making love" when they are not "making love" at all. To "make love" means to create through this action more love between us. But that can be done only if the action is a loving one, not a manipulation session or an achievement trip. And the action cannot "make love" if we've been at war throughout the day. Fifteen minutes of the mechanics manual's prescribed foreplay will not heal the wounds of fifteen hours of rudeness toward one's wife, or erase the harsh words thrown at her. No! Peace must be made before love can be made.

Some cynic once quipped: "Men will give love to get sex, women will give sex to get love." A cynic said it, and it isn't true. No mature woman can easily separate her sexual giving from her loving. It is when she knows she is loved, appreciated for herself, found desirable as the person she is, that she is most ready to give herself over to the man who so cares for her and wants her. And that is also why, when her husband begins to take her for granted, makes noises about her sexual desirability only when he is interested in sexual intercourse, or tells her he loves her only as a prelude to it, she becomes dissatisfied and—whatever his physical prowess—unhappy with him. This, in part, is what one woman meant by saying about the man she was divorcing: "He's great in bed, but he's a lousy lover."

We do well to remember that we are none of us victims of our histories. We are creators of ourselves. While we cannot expect to undo thirty-five or more years of miseducation in a few hours of reading, or by simply making up our minds, we can begin the task of working changes in our behavior right now. For if the ideas we have affect our behavior, it is likewise true that by changing behavior—and especially when we find the results rewarding—we can work changes in our attitudes. Improving our wife-wooing, for many of us in the middle years of our marriage, entails making such changes.

But there is another area that we ought to consider as we search for new life in our marriages: Have we met the woman who lives with us? Some haven't. One wife said of her husband: "He still introduces me as the brightest kid in our high school class, as though I hadn't done anything outstanding since then." Some are afraid to. "He won't talk to me of anything that really matters to me." Some don't think it would be worthwhile. "He is willing to talk and listen to anyone, male or female, about books, politics, movies—you name it. But when we're alone and I try to talk about a book I've read or offer some thought I've had, he just kind of mumbles and wanders off. I have the impression he doesn't think my thoughts are worth anything."

One of the basic signs of love is "paying attention." To pay attention to someone is to set aside your own thoughts, your own worries, seeing things from your own point of view, and—without thinking of what you're going to say in response, or without letting your mind wander—truly let the other be present for us. It is a laying down of our own lives for that space of time so that the other can live more abundantly in our presence. Many husbands would make some marvelous discoveries if they began to pay attention to their wives in this fashion; more importantly, they would be giving their wives new signs of their love.

One method, used by some therapists, to get husbands and wives to break out of their habitual ways of looking at each other is to have them sit and look at one another for five minutes in complete silence, with the instruction that they must try to see the other as if he or she just entered their lives. When couples do this, they are then asked to share their impressions of each other, their feelings about the experience. Some husbands might benefit by looking at their wives in that fashion, as if newly discovering them. Paying attention to the words and the personality of the other as she is now is one further step in advancing our love affair. Another might be to put our creative energies into "making time" with the other. When I was in high school, "making time" meant enhancing a relationship with a girl, and I mean to imply something of that special sense here. Again and again, I meet marriage situations in which the couple speaks of "not finding time." "Just can't find the time."

I have never yet stumbled across twenty minutes lying on the sidewalk, though once I found a twenty dollar bill. Nor have I ever met anyone who just happened across two weeks of time somebody had left in the park I doubt that anyone else has done so either, for the simple reason that time is not *found.* Time is created by us for the things we want to do. It often requires conscious planning to create those chunks of time we can devote totally to the other.

I know of one San Francisco husband who tried for three months to get away for a weekend with his wife. Each scheduled date was demolished by something that took precedence: foreign visitors arriving, a sick child, a relative's death. Undaunted, he took a weekday off from work and, after the children were sent off to school, took his wife out for a breakfast of Eggs Benedict and champagne at a Sausalito restaurant where they could dine on an outside deck overlooking San Francisco Bay. Then they strolled the streets, visited the shops and galleries, where he bought a gift for her. Returning to the city, he took her boating on the lake in Golden Gate Park. They had tea in the Japanese Tea Garden and returned home in time to see to the organization of the children's supper, to change, and to go out for dinner. Later they went somewhere for an after-dinner drink, and then, before returning home, they took a stroll along the shore in the moonlight.

That was created time. It was a time "made" by him for their mutual enjoyment and personal, intimate dialogue. This was a couple married eighteen years and he was still determinedly "making time." His creative energies, however, went not only into creating time, but creating the day, for all the planning was done by him. He presented his wife with the day. One woman, told of this, commented: "Imagine receiving a day for a present. Why, it's beyond price."

There are other creative uses of time. What about creating the conditions necessary to free one's wife so that she can do something for her personal pleasure and enrichment? I know of a woman who became a radiologist and a grandmother in the same year. If she did the former through her own evening class and summer session efforts, her husband was a major collaborator in this creation of herself as a skilled professional. He helped create the time and the conditions necessary for her to grow in this fashion. They had six children living at home when she began her schooling, so much of his creative effort was put into housework and childcare after he came in from his own work. Wearing an apron and doing the dishes didn't threaten him a bit, because he was a mature man who knew that he was loved by a mature woman. Her growth, as his, contributes to their growth; they are not in competition with one another, but are strengthening and helping one another.

Many husbands resent any interests or hobbies their wives have that are independent of their own. In so doing, they reveal their basic insecurities. At the same time, they are depriving themselves of sharing in their spouses' increased joy in life. The husband who wants to show his love for his wife will be supportive of her independence as a person. He will also be aware of her need for times of privacy; times to be alone to read, to meditate, or just to be silent. Some husbands intrude on such times with "What are you thinking?" and get resentful if the other dismisses this intrusion with an "Oh, nothing." It might be useful to remind ourselves that we speak to one another out of our silences, that I bring to you only what I have gained for myself. We need to help create for our spouse those spaces of time devoted to selfing—to becoming a richer person by doing what she enjoys doing. That may mean a husband baby-sitting or, if the children are grown, merely pursuing his own goals while his wife takes belly dancing or yoga, goes on retreat or attends evening classes.

Every marriage is a unique creation. That is why it is difficult to offer specific counsel in making advances in the love affair, in rooting out the routine in sex. The difficulty is that some individuals might take a sort of guideline suggestion and apply it as mechanically and manipulatively as any they had previously found in the mechanics manual of sex. Instead of improving their personal expressions of love, they would merely be substituting a new script. It is crucial that any husband interested in becoming a better lover, realize that the love relationship—that twenty-four-hour-a-day sexual relationship—is the key factor and not some esoteric bedroom tactic. In looking to enhance the relationship, to break out of routines, to bring new life and new energies into the marriage, it is necessary to look to one's personal style and one's wife's needs, and to use one's imagination creatively. Not long ago, one husband stopped at the grocery store on the way home from work and bought some steaks, potatoes, a bottle of wine, and some charcoal. He arrived home, told his wife to grab some warm clothes and he threw the sleeping bags in the station wagon. "What's going on?" she asked.

"I've decided to run away with you," he replied. He drove her to a nearby state park, where they enjoyed their steaks and wine and a night under the stars. Later he said, "She told me she was feeling cooped up, so I decided to take her out of the coop."

That sort of "surprise," however, may be just the wrong sort for your wife if she, for example, hates camping, doesn't like steaks and doesn't drink wine. But that sort of response to the other's needs—whatever form it may take —is a loving response.

A final word is in order about sexual activity in the middle and later years. What needs to be stated most forcefully, and can be stated without equivocation, is that there is no physical or biological reason why men and women should, as they age, stop having sexual intercourse. Cultural conditioning and old wives' tales are the principal causes of older people foregoing it; some feel they are expected to, they themselves expect to, and the expectation is self-fulfilling.

Biological changes do occur as we age, of course. Our physical stamina is not what it might have been at twenty or twenty-five. We can't now necessarily duplicate our track and field or football feats of college days. Aware of that, we ought not to be surprised at our noting some effects of middle age on our sexual responses. As Masters and Johnson's research and therapeutic experience have indicated, the biological changes that occur in the male after the onset of middle age might make him slower to gain an erection, and the erection may not be as firm as when he was younger. However, the same factors contribute to his being able to continue intercourse for a longer period of time prior to ejaculation. He may find, as he passes fifty, that his penis becomes flaccid much more rapidly after ejaculation than it did in his younger years and that it may take him longer to regain his erection. These slowdowns in physical response are one with the general slowdown we all experience as we grow older. They do not constitute any barriers to sexual intercourse. Indeed, particularly in providing the male with a longer period of actual sexual intercourse prior to ejaculation, they very often mean that the wife finds her sexual pleasure increased and her husband a better lover than ever before. This is particularly true if the wife was previously slow in reaching a climax.

Further, men in their middle years often try to suppress or control their breathing during the sexual act and during and after orgasm. As one man put it, "I don't want to sound like a beached whale." For the most part, this is an effort to conceal weakness and is rooted in the mistaken notions, already mentioned, of athleticism. This effort to avoid sounding winded deprives the blood of the oxygen it needs and which the body is demanding. That deprivation of proper oxygenation means that the man fatigues more quickly and is less prepared to have a second erection.

It might also be beneficial for us to remember that nearly every man prematurely ejaculates at some time or another. Nearly every man is occasionally impotent. And just about every man among us was given wrong attitudes about women and sex as we were growing up. Having said that much, let me reiterate that it is the reduction of our thinking about our sexual relationship to a matter of the genitals alone that has been the major single hang-up of American men and has brought about much of the misery about sexual matters that men and women suffer today.

So let's leave athleticism to the athletes on the playing fields, performance to performers, and the nonsense of our past in the past. Let's begin to make some new attempts to get to know the woman with whom we are living. Let's seek some new ways of showing our spouse that we love her and appreciate her womanly presence in our lives twenty-four hours a day.

And when we're in bed together, or on the livingroom rug, or wherever we may happen to be lying side by side, let's just relax and enjoy one another's company and follow the natural flow of our intimacy, remembering that our sexuality is expressed in our total physical being and not just in the genitals. Touching, caressing, kissing, providing a sensuous massage, all have their own loving message to convey and can be enjoyed for their own sake rather than as preludes to full sexual exchange.

We may—by putting renewed energies into our wife-wooing—begin to discover that loving one another and being together in that love is what the sexual act is all about. And when we make that discovery, we're beginning the first day of all the years of the best time of our lives.

CHAPTER V

A TIME
TO LOVE

On my fortieth birthday my wife surprised me with a party attended by numerous friends. As the evening ended and guests were leaving, Fred took me aside. Fred is a soft-spoken man, married, the father of three. A technician by trade, he is also an omnivorous reader and has written for publication from time to time. He is as stable as any man I know and far more sensitive than most. "I was forty just three years ago," he said that night. "When my friends told me then that I'd be experiencing everything from near despair to a roving eye, I laughed at them. I didn't believe a word of it. But I thought I'd better warn you; it's all true, every bit of it. For me it was worse than they predicted—and it's not over yet. Just don't let it overwhelm you."

Social psychologist Marjorie Fiske Lowenthal describes middle age as "a crisis very much like the crisis of adolescence." Like that earlier adolescence, it can be for a man a period of uncertainties and inner questionings, of fears and strange stirrings. Looking into the mirror, he may see a face more closely resembling his father's than the one he'd come to accept as his. There's no longer any denying the grey which is now more predominant than the youthful color of his hair. The co-worker or close friend who drops dead of a heart attack at forty-four may cause him to experience pangs about his own mortality. He realizes that even should he be spared a coronary or an auto accident, the actuarial tables place him at over the half-way mark through life, with fewer years ahead of him than are already behind him. In his office he sees men only ten years older than himself being pushed into early retirement to make room for the younger men who seem to fill the building. He was thirty-three when he got promoted to the job now held by a twenty-seven-year-old. In a variety of ways he is becoming acutely aware of his aging and may consciously contrast his youthful hopes of achievement with what, in fact, he has achieved in life.

If his strivings have brought him to the "American Dream" goal of his depression-survivor parents—a home of his own, two cars, enough income to provide many small and not so small luxuries, including giving the kids all that he did not have in the way of material gifts—he may be come more depressed than his less successful brothers Much depends upon the degree to which he believed the national myth that economic success and the commodities it enabled him to purchase would bring him a strong sense of personal well-being and enrich his family's happiness. Often enough, his very devotion to material goals has taken its toll, strained the marital relationship itself, left him bereft of intimate contact with his children—to whom he gave things instead of giving himself.

Bewildered by the failure of success to fulfill its promises, he may also feel trapped in his present situation. His status, and his wife's status among their peers, rests upon his maintaining his present position. Even if he no longer likes his work, he may feel unfree to change it. After all, he's devoted years to this work, is experienced in it. Even if the unemployment picture was not already grimly peopled with salesmen and middle-aged executives, what else can he earn a living at but what he is doing now? Confronted by the need to increase his income annually just to maintain his family's present standard of living in these inflationary times, he continues to strive to meet that need even though he may be disillusioned by the contrast between his youthful aspirations and the present day reality.

Awareness of aging, the hollow ring of success, the sense of being ensnared by circumstances, the slowdown of some bodily responses, and other factors—singly or in combination—can cause an inner turmoil of self-doubt, questionings, tensions, conflicting feelings. And it is just these feelings that most American men are ill-equipped to cope with.

As a child, the American male was in various ways conditioned not to display weakness, but to be aggressive and "tough." Men, we were taught, were displaying weakness when they showed themselves vulnerable in some way, gave expression to tenderness or sensitivity, or demonstrated some emotional need. The cowboy riding off alone into the sunset, leaving behind the girl who loved him; the tight-lipped Gary Cooper or the gruff-voiced John Wayne; the hard guy, Humphrey Bogart; these were some of the role models for the growing boy. More importantly, in the precincts of his home and daily life, he was taught that expressing pain was unmanly. "Big boys don't cry." Tears were for "sissies,"—that is, girls like his sister.

In his manhood, he comes to look upon his male peers as his competitors in the status struggle. At work his subordinates are functionaries to whom he must always appear to be in control of the situation; and his chances for advancement might be jeopardized if his superiors find him in any way unsure of himself. He has great difficulty expressing his true feelings to his own wife, let alone to his best male friends. More than one wife has been astonished to learn that her husband and his best friend have spent the day golfing or fishing together and did not discuss the friend's marital problems, which, she has learned from the other's wife, have reached the breaking-up point. The sort of intimate exchange many women take for granted is unusual among most men because they have been conditioned to believe that it is "unmanly" to share their emotional problems, or that such sharing would weaken their image in the eyes of the other. In fact, because he has so long avoided sharing his inner life with others, has become so accustomed to suppressing this aspect of his nature, he may have great difficulty sorting out what it is that he does truly feel.

Suffering the stress of these emotional crosscurrents of middle age with little or slight insight into what is troubling him, he may try to "tough it out," to behave as if he is not hurting. The tactic seldom works, for the feelings still seek some outlet. No man decides: "My youthful dreams haven't been realized, therefore I will drink more heavily and drown my miseries." No husband reasons: "I feel trapped and I resent it. I can't express that at the office, so I will get angry with my wife over tonight's meal." Nor does he conclude: "I've worked hard for success and my wife and children don't appreciate how hard or we'd be happier, therefore I will withdraw." Least of all does he tell himself: "I feel unmanned, I'm unsure of my virility these days. I will reassure myself by making a play for that girl in the accounting department." No. Ill at ease on the restless sea of his personal feelings, he clings to the liferaft of his work, no matter how flimsy it may now appear to him, and is tossed this way and that by the undercurrents, sometimes lapsing into behavior as perplexing to himself as it is wounding to his spouse.

Perhaps at no other time in his life have his inner resources, his spiritual strengths, been so tested. The atheist who has a strong sense of his own self worth, is aware of the value of persons, and has some understanding of what love may require, will surely weather the crisis better than the Sunday churchgoer whose credo is but a string of words that have never informed his life. Both of these, as well as the truly prayerful man, the college professor, and the housepainter—in short, almost all men—are confronting the reality of their aging and probably experiencing one fear or another that they've never before felt.

The "crisis of middle age" for a husband may or may not coincide with his wife's menopausal years. Granted that few women today seem to dread the menopause as they did only a generation or two ago, it is nonetheless a time of profound change for them. The period of transition has been eased from the physical standpoint by various medical advances; but more important, perhaps, is the attitudinal change. Women today do not look upon the end of their childbearing years as tantamount to the loss of womanhood, but, on the contrary, as a release from the inconveniences of menstruation and worries about pregnancy.

Whether or not she has yet entered her menopausal years, today's woman of middle years has not been prematurely aged by the heavier maintenance and survival chores that burdened her predecessors. Having, generally speaking, ended her childbearing years at an earlier age than previous generations of women, she finds herself at this time of her life with more time and energy to devote to pursuits chosen by herself rather than those imposed upon her by her role as wife and mother. Many a woman who had previously immersed herself almost totally in providing supportive encouragement to her husband's career and meeting the manifold time- and energy-consuming demands of bearing and raising young children, has begun to feel new and deeper needs for understanding, emotional intimacy, supportive encouragement for herself. She may also have begun to make other changes in her personal life style, asserting herself more than in the past, developing talents or professional skills she had permitted to lie dormant for years.

It is not uncommon for her to be surprised, appalled, even deeply hurt by the reaction of her husband to her new assertions of herself. If she does not comprehend the sources from which her husband's reactions flow, she may aggravate the situation further rather than work toward the renewal of their relationship which she seeks. Two wives, Ruth and Susan, were doing just that.

Ruth and Martin were married when they were eighteen. Today at forty, they are a handsome, even a striking couple with more than average intelligence, abounding energy, and contagious enthusiasms. During the early years of their marriage—as Martin moved from smaller to larger successes in his career—Ruth enjoyed the experiences of pregnancy and the motherhood of their three children. These were years marked by a keen sense of sharing and mutual delight for both Ruth and Martin. Their youngest child is now fifteen. Martin's talents have brought him enough recognition that his picture appeared recently in a national magazine. Their friends consider them a well-matched and even an ideal couple.

Ruth is not happy, however. She says: "I can't get him to see that I am no longer the hero-worshipping eighteen-year-old I was when we married. I'm a mature woman now and I have personal needs, emotional needs that go beyond the roles of mothering, being a charming hostess, catering to his moods. He tells me I'm just having an off day, or that I've been reading too much fem lib propaganda, or he simply says he doesn't know what I'm talking about. That is, when I get a chance to talk about my feelings at all. We never go out alone anymore. Most of the time, even at home, he's got people to be entertained. Other times he says he's too busy with his latest project or too tired to talk sensibly. He's great at coming up with excuses for ducking the issue. I don't want a separation or a divorce, but he may drive me to it unless our relationship improves."

Paralleling this somewhat is Susan's experience with Michael. A statuesque forty-one-year-old woman, Susan keeps in trim by diet and exercise. She says: "Our honeymoon was a sexual disaster. I'd have divorced him in the first six months if it hadn't been for our religious beliefs. Then, as children came along, we got involved in church work, settling into a new home, and child care. I buried my feelings. My life was a half-filled cup and I sought to fill it by living for the cleanest house, the most satisfied kids, the most perfect evening meal. I took to watching soap operas for some sort of emotional life. I felt guilty because I wasn't happy with what I had. After all, he's as reliable as Old Faithful, doesn't get drunk, seldom complains, loves the children—though he doesn't discipline them at all—and, in his way, loves me. I went through years of reciting that litany to myself and tried to be grateful; but I wasn't happy.

"In the last few years I reached the point where I knew I couldn't be content with the crumbs of intimacy he tossed me, with spending all of my time meeting the needs of others and having so little attention paid to my own. I quit the church activities. I told him they were an 'escape' for us, and I wanted time for myself, for us. He continued to carry them on, though. He's a bit ashamed of me about that, I think, and he doesn't really give me any more of his time than before. Then I began to see that I had helped to create the situation I was in and I began to try to change that by asserting myself more, making demands, telling him outright of my unhappiness. I wanted us to get into therapy, but he said we couldn't afford it and it conflicted too much with his own schedule. So now I'm in an all-women therapy group. I don't sit still for anything any longer. I make demands upon him that I never used to make. He follows through on some, but he's not really there. He does it to keep me happy, without grasping what it's all about. I almost left him last summer. That's a scary prospect to me. But unless things change, I'm going to have to leave in order to save my life."

"In what way do you want him to change?" I asked.

"Humanly. He's just got to relate to me on a more human, a more personal level. I'm a full grown woman with needs for emotional closeness, for personal warmth, for the appreciation of myself as a person that I'm not getting from him."

"And are your demands usually verbalized?"

"Yes."

"How does he respond to these verbal demands?"

"He withdraws even further. He behaves as if I'm unreasonable. Sometimes he sulks. He does anything but meet me where I'm at."

"But he doesn't argue much or get into intense discussions with you, or talk about where he's coming from?"

"No. God, if he would! Even that would be an opening, a human contact. He usually fires some parting shot and goes into his shell. Recently I told him I felt I was married to a turtle."

These women have different religious and cultural backgrounds, live in different parts of the state, have never met; but they all share the desire to bring new life to their marriages, and they confront husbands who are resisting their efforts. Whatever form that resistance takes, it is coming from a man beset by the inner uncertainties and fears already described, who is often doing his very best to cope. He may even be coping fairly adequately, in his own eyes, for he is used to confronting those demands in the familiar areas of his business and social life. Now, to find his wife enunciating new demands upon him unsettles him further.

He may even feel it is a bit unfair. Home is where he should be accepted for himself as he is—in his own eyes a good husband, good father, good provider. He now finds his adequacy being challenged here, too. Not only do these new demands come at the very time when doubts about himself, his goals, his life's worth have begun to press upon him, but they are more frightening than any of the others. For his wife is asking him to share more of himself, to find new emotional sources in himself, to show new strength in their love relationship just when he feels most weak. She is asking for greater intimacy at a time when he feels most vulnerable. The more afraid he is of being seen by her as inadequate, the more forcefully he may resist her efforts. He may never have appeared so cold to her, so inhuman and unfeeling toward her, so unconcerned about their relationship. Yet his behavior results very often from the reverse facts: that he has never before felt himself so totally human, so vulnerable, so inadequate, and he fears the loss of her love if she discovers him in that condition.

Since she is his wife, her expressed dissatisfaction strikes right to the core of his identity: his sexuality. For it is precisely as her husband, her lover, her man, that she is asking something more of him than what he has so far given. For some men, trapped by their conditioning, the reactions of Martin and of Michael are their forms of resistance. They try to maintain the status quo by not confronting the issue. Devoting increasing amounts of time to work is another common method of avoiding the issue. Some seek refuge in heavy drinking and belligerant behavior, in the adolescent notion that these are assertions of their being "he-men." Still others seek personal validation of their masculinity, their sexual desirability, by turning their attentions to other women. Some even flaunt such escapades before their wives as if they were certificates of their "manliness."

All such resistance, of course, only increases the alienation, the estrangement in the marriage. The wife who wishes to avoid such an outcome as she seeks to bring new life to her marital relationship has need, then, to ground her efforts in a recognition of what her husband may himself be going through at this time. Both Ruth and Susan were taking their husband's reactions at face value. In touch with their own feelings, knowing what they wanted, able to articulate those needs, they assumed their husbands' reactions were rooted in similar self-knowledge and similar freedom to verbalize. From what has already been said about the masculine mystique and the male crisis in middle age, we can see that this usually isn't the case. It is much more likely that the dissatisfied wife is confronting a man whose need for deeper understanding is equivalent to her own but whose burden is heavier because, unlike her, he finds it almost impossible to share with anyone else what is troubling him.

Oftentimes a wife blames herself, or fears there is something wrong in the marriage relationship, when the cause of the problem lies elsewhere. One woman—call her Marilyn—found her husband loving in all sorts of ways; he was very considerate of her and they did a lot of things together. He was a wonderfully thoughtful companion. However, he had almost given up initiating lovemaking. It had become a matter of once a month, rarely twice. Blaming herself for this, she sought to dress more attractively for him, provide more "romantic" moments, but he didn't seem to respond. Even direct attempts at seduction failed because, at those times, he couldn't sustain an erection.

Discussion with the husband brought out that he was having job problems. Cutbacks on the work force had nearly doubled his work load and he was putting forth extraordinary energies to meet those demands because he feared the next cutback might include him. Worried about the loss of his job and what that would mean to them, he was suffering at the same time from fatigue. He hadn't shared his worries with Marilyn because, he said, "I love her and I didn't want her worrying. I want her happy."

Once Marilyn was confronted with the true source of her husband's seeming lack of interest, she was able to see that her direct approach to the problem of their conjugal intercourse had only been placing another demand for performance upon him, adding to his stress situation. She was advised to get him to share his concerns with her while they were in bed, to prompt him to talk out some of his worries and fears, and to provide him with her loving reassurance. She was also counseled to get a book on sensual massage and to use physical techniques for relaxing him physically, easing some of his tensions. Through closeness of this sort they might find themselves giving full physical expression to their love; but that was not the immediate goal. Otherwise the "bed talk" and the massage would be mere ploys instead of loving times worthwhile for their own sakes. The "bed talk" and the helps to physical relaxation were both aimed at alleviating to some degree the inner stress and bodily fatigue that were debilitating him. Once these were alleviated, the matter of sexual lovemaking moved into its proper place as an expression of their intimacy.

Had she not had this sort of counsel, Marilyn might well have shifted from blaming herself—having made every effort at making herself attractive and trying to arouse him sexually—to blaming him and expressing her sentiments openly That new burden of blame would have compounded his problem greatly. His anxiety about failure at work would have been joined by guilt over having failed Marilyn at home.

Ruth and Susan, in continuing to take a demanding approach to their husbands, only further aggravated their withdrawal. Marilyn, too, had been moving along a path toward furthering the very situation she wanted to improve.

For another woman, Janet, the problem and the appropriate response were quite different from Marilyn's. In her late thirties, Janet would sit slumped in a chair, her eyes downcast. Even when she raised them, they lacked life's sparkle; they were signal flags calling for pity. It was obvious that she had given little attention to her makeup or her clothes, though her high cheekbones and large eyes gave indications of a woman who could be attractive if she chose. Her face was expressionless, as drained of strength as her voice, which was a dull monotone inflected occasionally by what can only be described as a whine.

"He stays away from home so much," she said. "I never know whether he'll be there for dinner or not. He works late all the time and when he leaves work, he goes drinking with an old army buddy, or else he goes alone. On weekends he goes back to his shop to work, or he goes fishing with his friend or to a ball game."

"How do you spend your time when he's away?"

"I seem to spend all of my time waiting for him these days."

"When he does come home, what do you do?"

"I ask him where he's been. I tell him how unhappy I am about the way he's treating me. I beg him to change."

"How does he respond to this?"

"If he's been drinking, he gets angry and we quarrel. If he's not been drinking, he just tells me I'm his wife, not his keeper. I usually end up crying myself to sleep. We've made love twice in the last year and he was drunk both times."

Janet was asked to close her eyes and to imagine herself as Pete, her husband, who operates his own small garage.

He loves working on automobiles, has done so since high school. It is five o'clock and he can quit work now and go home or he can work on another car awaiting his attention. He thinks of going home.

Having been gently led to place herself in her husband's stead, Janet was now asked to visualize herself as he sees her at this moment of decision. "Now, put that image you have of Janet into words."

She was silent for a while, then the words began to come haltingly. "Janet's waiting. She looks tired, beaten. She's got no energy. She hasn't even put on any lipstick today. She's unhappy.

"What do you feel about this, Pete?" she was asked.

Her eyes still closed, Janet responded: "I enjoy my work; I like what I'm doing. I'm depressed now at the thought of seeing her. I don't want to see her. She makes me feel guilty."

"What do you do, Pete?"

"I go over and lift the hood on the other car." With that Janet opened her eyes.

Janet now saw—with open eyes—that she had been contributing heavily to the very situation that was making her unhappy. Once she saw that, she was receptive to looking at the wide range of options available to her for eliciting the changes she wanted: her husband's love, his respect, his presence.

Janet did have, after all, time. Moreover, she had the freedom to choose how she would spend her time. She had been using her freedom and time only to wait for her husband's arrival to confront him with her miserable self. But she could go swimming, join a bowling league, play tennis, attend courses at a local college, get a part-time job, do volunteer work. She might start by treating herself to the luxury of an afternoon at a beauty salon for the full treatment. She could follow, in short, her personal inclinations with regard to enriching herself physically, intellectually, emotionally, spiritually, even financially.

Then, when Pete came home, he'd be meeting a person

with ideas and enthusiasms. And unless he had specified that he would be home for dinner, she could quit manufacturing the personal disappointment of making a dinner for him that would only get cold. Janet was also advised to forego whimpering about his tardiness and instead to show her delight that he had arrived. Surely she could provide a greeting for him that he'd prefer to working on a greasy motor or to the slap on the back from his drinking buddy.

By working changes in her own attitudes and her approach to the problem, she would be working toward the goal she desired: a husband more eager to be in her company. Even were that response not immediately forthcoming, she still would be immeasureably happier with herself. Also, she would be growing out of the almost total emotional and psychological dependency she had on him at the time: a dependency she created and had been perpetuating.

Between the attempts to improve verbal communications and the seeking of professional help for improving the marital relationship lie many other options. The advice given Janet is something many wives might benefit from: to devote some energies to working changes in themselves, changes which expand their personal sense of well-being.

Often enough, upon discovering that there is "another woman," wives ask themselves: "What's she got that I haven't?" At the risk of oversimplification, what she very often has is that she's someone new. Because she displays abilities or talents or qualities as a person that are not seen in the wife, she attracts interest.

To the degree that any wife undertakes the effort to enhance herself, not only in the superficial way of clothes and makeup but in terms of the expression of her personality and the exercise of her talents, she reveals a new person to her spouse. This selfing effort might include anything from learning a new skill to dusting off an old ambition and setting about its accomplishment. It may be as simple as deciding upon a regular regimen of exercise at a spa, or as complex as deciding to become a licensed realtor. What is important is that it is time and effort devoted to tapping one's own potential for personal growth. The energies thus unleashed further enhance one's whole being and, by so doing, mean that they call forth new responses from those around us. "She's become a new woman since she discovered politics," said one admiring husband of his wife. By becoming a "new woman" she had elicited new responsiveness toward herself as a person.

Oftentimes "the other woman" has as her main attraction only a seemingly keener interest in him as he is now, giving expression to full appreciation of the good qualities that seem to be taken for granted by his wife. Some wives, indeed, haven't taken a good look at their husbands in years. It might be a good exercise for a wife to try to get a fresh and impartial view of her husband, to look upon him as a person who has just entered her life this day. She might do what she did when they were courting: express interest in him as a person, share reminiscences, ask questions that help him to express his sense of where he's at, all with that attentiveness, that "good listener" approach she has at her command. If she could see him with new eyes, as some other woman might view him, she might come to a deeper appreciation of his uniqueness. And that new appreciation might lead her to become, in a sense, "the other woman," seeking new and imaginative ways to communicate her love.

In most cases there is nothing to prevent a wife from taking the initiative in offering surprises, planning evenings or weekends that would add to their mutual enjoyment. Yet many a wife has fallen into the habit of leaving such initiative up to her husband and, when he doesn't act, resenting the fact that the days are barren of such delights. By taking such initiative—whether sending a love letter to his office, presenting a surprise gift at dinner, or some other appropriate gesture—she is taking creative steps that show her husband how much she appreciates him, and it may stimulate him to reciprocate. It is important that all such gestures be rooted in an authentic love for the other or they are

hollow of meaning, mere shallow stratagems that will ultimately fail.

Often a wife may find that taking the first step in changing behavior in the areas of minor irritation brings immediate reward. The wife, leaving a restaurant with her husband
and seeing the man ahead of them putting his arm around
his own wife, may feel cheated that her husband doesn't
express his closeness to her in that particular way. She
might nurture that moment of resentment, adding it to
dozens of other such negative moments that increase her
discontent. On the other hand, she could take the initiative
of saying simply: "That looks nice," and put her own arm
about her husband's waist. There can be no doubt which
alternative is the one that leads nowhere and which is a
creative response to her own felt need—a need she has
taken immediate steps to satisfy.

Positive suggestions made in specific terms are more
liable to tap the potential for change than mere complaints.
"We never do anything together anymore," is a negative
comment that may, even if it avoids argument, lead nowhere in particular. "I've been thinking. Let's arrange our
Saturdays so that we can play tennis together. I'd really
enjoy that and we both could use the exercise," is a positive
proposal open to immediate adoption as a plan of action.

Ruth came to recognize that her "demands" for Martin
to change were getting nowhere, to be aware also that her
attempts to communicate on a deeper level with him were
constantly short-circuited by their hectic daily life. She
finally proposed: "Ernest and Sylvia have invited us to a
Marriage Experience Weekend coming up. I hear they're
beautiful, restful, and fun and I'd like us to go." Martin
probably would not have come up with this suggestion
himself, nor would he have willingly gone had Ruth blud-
geoned him with: "There's a Marriage Experience Weekend coming up and, by God, we need something to help
us communicate." By switching from her "demands"
to a positive approach, Ruth made it easier for Martin to
accept. In the context of this weekend devoted to private

husband/wife dialoguing, Martin and Ruth rediscovered one another and made the first step toward moving their marriage to a new level of intimacy.

Sometimes all that is required is that a wife cease to collaborate in the creation of her own areas of resentment. The wife who resents having to decide for her husband when he should have his haircut ("He asks me if he needs one? He does this in all sorts of things. You'd think I was his mother.") can simply refuse to tell him. "That's your decision, not mine." Or: "I don't know. Don't you know?" He may resist this, but the wife who persists in her refusal to collaborate in this "mothering," will have forced him to take some responsibility for his own person, and will also have removed one source of irritation in the relationship.

Another wife described her refusal to cooperate in her own unhappiness. "I had lived for years by the dictum that 'a good wife never says no.' I don't accept that anymore. I don't accept less than the best. A bit of breast-fondling when we're getting ready for bed doesn't make up for a day of being unpleasant, and I say so. And when he's drunk and wants to, I tell him I'm not his whore and I don't make love to drunks. I used to put up with that sort of thing—and I hated him for it and I hated myself for it. I no longer put up with it and I like myself better and I like him more. I expect more of him now than I ever did—and he delivers. It's because I see that my whole past was one that diminished me, that said I was there to be used when he wished. Well, no more. Sex is something we do together, me wanting it as well as him, or not at all."

This woman's experience is her own. Her husband, like herself, is a unique person; their relationship is different from any other marriage. Therefore, no general rule can be made out of her response to her situation. Still, there is a worthwhile insight to be gleaned from her experience. Having collaborated in experiences that were demeaning to her and thereby diminished her self-esteem and her esteem for her husband, she asserted her dignity as a human being. She let him know that she expected better of both herself and him. Most of us, in fact, do live up to (or down to) the expectations of those we love. Her husband was not an exception to this. By her elevation of her expectations of him, a change was wrought in their sexual patterns. It was turned from a one-sided experience, which many times was a source of bitterness to her, into one of mutuality. By her own statement, she likes her husband and herself more as a result.

Very often in this realm of sexual activity we find the symptoms of a breakdown in personal intimacy. The sexual act is a communications medium that speaks of where the couple is at as a couple, what they mean to one another, who they are to one another. If we are spiritually divorced, if we engage in the act despite a day of being unpleasant, or when one partner is drunk, the act is hollow of meaning. One partner is using the other or we are performing a meaningless routine; or perhaps we are actually lying to one another, engaging in an act that speaks of love when we are feeling unloving. The sexual act is at its qualitative best when it communicates mutual love.

It does more than that, however. We often hear the term "lovemaking" used about the sexual act. Unfortunately, the term is so loosely used as a synonym for sexual activity that it does not always describe the reality of the specific situation. However, it is an action which is capable of doing just that: "making" love between the couple. That is why it is unwise to withdraw from sexual activity because of tensions in the relationship. The sexual act itself can become a source of deeper intimacy, can create more love between the couple.

As for the continuation of sexual activity as she grows older, the woman, like the man, experiences hormonal changes that cause some slight shifts in the sexual response and the anatomy. It may take a few minutes longer for the wife to become lubricated. Her clitoris, while still responding to stimulation, may get smaller. Her experience of orgasm may be shorter than when she was younger, with fewer vaginal and uterine contractions discernible. If she experiences, during or after menopause, any problems such as bleeding from the vaginal wall, her doctor can usually relieve such by hormonal treatments, for it is the cutback in hormonal production at this time which is usually the source of such problems. Many women never require any such hormonal replacement in order to continue to enjoy a high level of sexual responsiveness as they grow older.

What needs to be said—because there continues to be amazing ignorance about such things—is that there is for the normal woman no reason she should ever have to consider the days of her enjoyment of sexual activity at an end merely because she has reached a certain age.

But what of the wife who is aware of this, who desires to have the full expression of love but finds her husband's invitations to do so coming less often? We have, in the last chapter, talked directly to the husbands about this. A wife might in this regard look to herself. If she has been too passive during lovemaking, he may have become discouraged about his ability to arouse her. If she has permitted the times between his invitations to lengthen without herself taking any lovemaking initiatives, he may feel that she can "take it or leave it." Indeed, he may even feel less attractive to her. Many women, because of their upbringing, do leave all such initiatives up to their husbands and are seemingly unaware that—especially at times when he is already depressed or feeling cut off for reasons described earlier—he may need just such affirmations of his manly attractiveness as some initiatives from her would give.

At the time we married, both men and women were being told that the feminine orgasm was the mark of the successful lover. "There are no frigid women," one phrase of that time went, "only inadequate men." But orgasm was defined in such a fashion that few women ever knew the experience: from Hemingway's "the earth moved" to poetic raptures and swoons of ecstasy. But orgasmic response varies widely in the same woman from one experience to another, just as the levels of orgasmic pleasure in the man can vary. If her husband looks each time for some profound response—as a sign he has succeeded—a wife might reassure and educate him to the fact that she can be perfectly content with the very pleasant experience she has just had.

The search for orgasm that engaged the attention of so many men and women for so long was a search which often diverted them from the true gold that was in their daily experience. In fact, the anxiety produced by that search—as he struggled to produce it in her, to validate his manhood, and as she struggled to achieve it—was often the reason for their dissatisfaction and even dysfunction.

When, a few years back, the goal was changed to simultaneous orgasm, many lovers made the mistake of seeking to win this new trophy. Again, the orgasm was made the goal of the sexual encounter and all else that it has to offer was subordinated or lost in the attempt to achieve that goal. Simultaneous orgasm, it can be argued, is less pleasurable than those enjoyed in succession. For in the latter each has the pleasure of experiencing the other's orgasmic response, while in the former both are so caught up in their own that the pleasure in the other's is lost.

At any rate, orgasm, whether individual or simultaneous, should be appreciated as part of a continuum in an event which is—taken in its totality—a symbol of our love and an intimate sharing of ourselves. The anxious strivings, rooted in our desire to prove our adequacies to ourselves or to the other, very often steal from us precisely what our sexual activity is supposed to bring to us: a greater intimacy, a more loving relationship.

Because husbands so often seem to isolate sexual activity from the totality of the love relationship, and because wives, generally speaking, cannot segregate sexual giving from loving, it may often fall to the wife to educate her husband into the paths of truly enriching sexual lovemaking, by some of the means mentioned and others that offer themselves to her.

All the foregoing remarks are but clues, examples indicative of more constructive approaches to bringing new life to the marital relationship. It cannot be stressed enough that we are not offering methods whereby one person manipulates another, but we are seeking to give ideas about more creative ways of expressing our own personal authentic needs. Because we are, each of us, unique, because every marriage relationship is unique, the ways of encouraging a husband's growth in love that may suit one woman's style of being, one marriage life style, may not be at all suitable for another.

Crucial to her bringing new life to their love relationship is the wife's understanding that she—precisely because she has been raised a woman—is probably much more keenly in touch with her own feelings, more at home with them, more capable of giving expression to them with emotional force than is her husband. She may be making a serious mistake if she interprets his withdrawal or resistance as a sign of his lack of love for her or lack of commitment to their marriage. Though in some cases this might be the fact, in most situations he is suffering the pangs of the middle-years crisis of the American male and may be hiding himself because he fears loss of her esteem if she should discover him in his wounded condition.

Because this period is often a time of unexpressed fears about himself and his adequacy, the means a wife chooses to enrich their relationship ought to be means that will not increase those fears but will work to their banishment through the power of that love which drives out fear. This does not mean, however, that the wife's role at this time is solely that of emotional nursemaid to her husband. No grown woman can respect for long a man who had need for her only, or primarily, in that way. It is to say that, as she strives to create a better marriage for herself, she should be conscious as well of his vulnerabilities, his needs. For it is only through that mutual awareness that the husband and wife, who are, after all, collaborators in the creation of their marriage, can work together toward a more living marriage.

CHAPTER VI

DAYS OF
GLADNESS

Marriage is not an "it" outside ourselves; nor is a marriage something that just happens to be good or bad or indifferent. Every marriage is a unique union of two unique human beings. But nearly all couples have experienced or are experiencing problems. How we cope with our marital difficulties—whether by surrender, flight, bitterness, behavior harmful to ourselves and others, or by confronting these as opportunities for advancing our love relationship—will depend to a great extent upon our own assumptions about the realities of love and marriage.

Perhaps the single most widespread error in contemporary thinking about marriage is that getting married to the one we love is, in itself, meant to bring us "happiness." The "and they got married and lived happily ever after" is a fairy-tale ending that bears little relationship to the reality of married living and loving.

That the happiness myth is still very much with us is evident in the oft-repeated comment made by those who attack marriage: "I know so few happy married couples." The power of the myth is felt by any of those who have to deal with people who opt for marriage as a solution to problems or as an escape hatch from present sufferings: teen-agers seeking a way out of the unhappiness of their parental homes; older persons looking to marriage to cure their loneliness or ease their sexual frustration; others looking for marriage to banish present unhappiness.

Marriage, however, brings no more guarantee of personal happiness than does celibacy or divorce or being a "swinging single." Indeed, realistic reflection upon human realities, our experience of life itself, ought to help us see that persons might have a very successful marital relationship and still not be happy people. Whatever the quality of our marital union, setbacks in work may render us unhappy, economic hardship may bring us worries, parental concerns or ill health may make laughter difficult for us. Consider the husband laboring to care for his children and at the same time pay the enormous costs of his wife's hospitalization. Their marital relationship is deep and unquestioned, but do we list them as "happily married" or "unhappily married"? Or is the happiness quotient, as a gauge of the quality of their personal relationship, irrelevant?

We need to remind ourselves that no state in life insures personal happiness. The fundamental commitment of human marriage is that two persons have chosen to share all of life's changes "for better or for worse, in sickness and in health," until death. That they've chosen to face life side by side does not exempt them from their share of those trials, tribulations, and times of unhappiness that all human beings experience. Persons who believe otherwise open themselves up to constant jolts throughout their married life as the real world, and the truth about life as it is lived, knock into their illusion. Yet, despite such jarring experiences, some of us continue to cling tenaciously to the myth. Marriage "promised" happiness. If we are not happy, it must be because we married the wrong person, that our spouse is not fulfilling his/her part of the bargain to make us happy. Even when they do not go the route of divorcing in order to lay the burden of making them "happy" upon someone else, people clinging to this myth often nourish feelings of resentment at life or the other partner. They display themselves as martyrs, or otherwise misuse the opportunities for growing up into knowing the satisfactions of a fully alive marriage.

Closely allied to the myth of happiness is the myth of marriage as somehow capturing for a lifetime the high erotic ardor of the couple's early infatuation. Even those who have a very successful marital relationship—a true companionship, intimacy, a mutual caring and friendship—may not recognize therein the features of mature loving, but yearn for the perfervid excitement, the adventure of that earlier love. Some women retreat to reading romances, some merely daydream and experience disappointment that their romantic fantasies bear so little relationship to daily life. Some men become cynical. Their remarks at weddings express their attitude that love is but the bait in a trap and the new groom will soon know a rude awakening. Members of either sex may look for that "romance" of the past in a liaison with a third party, where the clandestine nature of the relationship adds its own exotic element of adventure—at least in the beginning.

However expressed in words or actions by different people, the fact is that many of us do compare our present emotional life, vis-à-vis our spouse, with what we once experienced as "love" and are unsettled by the comparison. Indeed, the very comfortable nature of our relationship, our profound trust of each other, can become a source of discontent. "She takes me for granted." "Our life together is dull; there's no excitement in our relationship."

Others, less favored in the way of a harmonious relationship may be seeking the goal of "adjustment." To believe there is a moment in time when our differences will all be settled and our life from that point on will be one of harmony and peace, is to chase a will-o'-the-wisp and insure a succession of personal disappointments. Some of us, for example, believed that sexual adjustment was something we would achieve in the early months and years of our marriage. The scenario we envisioned saw us, after that period of adjustment, inhabiting a pleasure dome of mutual sexual fulfillment without any more difficulties or misunderstanding, the quality of our sexual activities now having been engineered to perfection. That there is no moment in a marriage when the couple can declare themselves now "adjusted"—sexually or otherwise—to each other, and henceforth live happily ever after, is simply one of the glorious truths of life.

For as long as we are alive, and as long as life offers us new challenges and disappointments, new pleasures and ideas, new responsibilities and worries, we ourselves will be growing and changing. We may adjust a motor, the thermostat on our furnace, the alarm on our clock, but we can never so adjust a human relationship. For human beings are profound mysteries, and we offer constant surprises even to ourselves in our ability to grow and change.

If I have taken the time to enumerate some of these major myths about marriage, it is because they can distract us from the truth. In so doing, they exert a strong negative influence upon marriages. Such erroneous assumptions about love and marriage—even when they do not lead to divorce—can sap our energies when we might otherwise have taken a more positive energetic part in creating our marriages. To nurture such myths, to continue to let them be operative in our lives, is to work against our own potential for increasing our delight and joy in our marital relationship.

Money, sex, the in-laws, disciplining the children, and other similar issues, usually lead the list of sources of marital breakdown. These problem areas, however, are just that: some of the problems married couples confront as they cope with daily life together. They may be severe problems, and sources of great tension or conflict, but they do not in themselves have the power to destroy a marriage. If the quality of our relationship is good, our mutual commitment to our marriage unquestioned, then the problems that we confront—even those that are sources of disagreement or disappointment between us—can become sources of a deeper loving. For to truly love another is to accept the other in his or her differences from oneself, to strive to understand the other's point of view, to forgive the other for transgressions against oneself, to seek to put the good of the other ahead of one's own self-seeking.

The talk of young lovers who express a willingness to endure any hardship for the beloved, even to die for the other, is romantic exaggeration; but it does point in the direction honest loving must take as it matures: the route of sometimes suffering for and perhaps because of the beloved, the route sometimes of a "little death" to self on one issue or another. It is precisely here that the quality of the love relationship is brought to the test. In such times love is challenged to grow more profoundly true to its nature: truer dedication to the good of the other and therefore to the relationship.

Some fail such tests by centering again on their own wills and withdrawing the gift of self. Others respond more generously and discover new strengths in their marriage as a result. In short, what matters most in any given marriage is not the problem the couple confronts but the attitudes they take toward the problem.

That is why the myths must be discarded, for they lead couples to confront even their smallest problems with the wrong attitudes, in the wrong spirit, in a negative or self-centered way. For all the myths have in common a strong emphasis upon personal gratification. The other is to make *me* happy. The other is to provide *me* with excitement or the sense of adventure in our marriage. The other is to fulfill *me* sexually. The myths also can seduce us into the false belief that, if not the other, then marriage itself is somehow at fault in our not having these unrealistic expectations fulfilled.

By this time it must be apparent that the fundamental insight being offered in these pages is that the responsibility for the quality of our marriage relationship is our own. Even the finest of professional counselors is powerless to aid a couple if they themselves refuse responsibility, decline to take action to improve their relationship. Most marriage counselors and therapists are well acquainted with couples who, after their initial session or two, after having laid out their problems, and the therapist has made some recommendations about changes that might benefit the marriage, do not return, or return with the report that they haven't followed the advice given. Such persons often seem to be seeking some instant cure, some miracle of words that will work the changes desired without any effort on their part. Some seem to prefer the pain of their present predicament to the pain of working some changes in their own behavior. Yet the price of freedom from continual dissatisfaction, the price of enhancing a relationship now lacking in vitality or pleasure is that we risk the pain of change.

Our contemporary climate is one that inspires people to flee from pain of any sort. Personal suffering is seen as an evil to be avoided at any cost. Many who ought to know better, believe that a life without any pain or anguish is possible. One can be wholeheartedly for the administration of anaesthesia and the alleviation of human miseries wherever they exist, and yet see as a gross misconception the notion that human life, human growth, human loving ought to be painless, that we ought to be able to live without any suffering. Consider for a moment the attitude we would take toward that person who suffered no pain when a child was injured; who felt no sorrow over the death of someone's dreams; who felt nothing, wept no tears, at the death of one he claimed to love; who suffered no guilt feelings at hurting another human being; who felt no pangs about his own inadequacies in loving, no hurt at being misunderstood or rejected. Would we, indeed, wish upon our worst enemy a life without such suffering? For not to suffer such things is to be inhuman. Our very humanity makes us open to a thousand such hurts. The very risk of loving another is that we open ourselves to suffering when the one we love suffers, and are vulnerable to what that one thinks of us, how that one behaves toward us.

It is often the case that the bond of husband and wife has been strengthened, the relationship made more mature and more vibrantly alive because of a suffering that was accepted, not passively—as the pain of deeper alienation or even the death of love—but actively, as a challenge to greater loving and deeper understanding of the other. Recently, I met a couple who had just weathered such a crisis. The husband, a dynamic and attractive salesman of forty, had for eighteen years been unfaithful to his wife. Because these infidelities always took place when he was on the road for his company, she knew nothing about them. His "one-night stands" in various cities always left him with heavy guilt feelings. In his words: "I hated myself for it." But that didn't stop him from his compulsive behavior at the next opportunity.

This man might have spent his life following this pattern, save that he got involved with a woman in his own city. This relationship grew into something more than the others and, in a burst of honesty, he told his wife that he desired a divorce in order to marry the other woman. Indeed, that evening he went to stay with her. His previous experiences also were divulged. The news was devastating to his wife. She, suffering more intensely than ever in her life, her pride crushed, her self-confidence as a woman shattered, briefly contemplated suicide. She dismissed the thought, however, and resolved that she would not permit this revelation to destroy her or her family. When next she saw her husband, she refused him the divorce he sought, demanding that he owed her and their teen-aged children the opportunity of seeing what could be done to save their relationship.

"I never felt closer to her, more in love with her, at any time since I met her as I did at that moment," he said. "And I agreed to seek counseling with her. I guess it was because I suddenly realized how deeply, how truly she loved me if she could know the truth about my behavior and still want to be married to me."

That incident had occurred two years before our meeting. Within weeks after entering counseling, he had stopped seeing the other woman and has been totally faithful to his wife since that time. "It was the most awful experience in my life," she said, "and yet our marriage today is better because of it. I've not entirely overcome the hurt to my self-esteem, but I do understand that it was something he would have done no matter who his wife was because it had to do with his own insecurities. He's worked these out now and he's so much happier with himself than he ever was before. And, of course, that makes me happier too. We've both grown up a lot. We don't play games and we're much freer with each other than ever before. I think today that we've got the best marriage of anyone we know. I mean it's really solid."

The husband added: "The only way I intend to leave this marriage is feet first."

A clergyman who knew the couple well and was acquainted with the situation commented later: "She was always the sort of woman you'd think of as 'very attractive,' but probably not notice after that. In the last two years she's become more than that, as you saw. There are these new depths to her personality that have made her extremely beautiful and so very womanly. I never see her lately that I don't think she's a walking example of the redemptive value of suffering."

Whatever the value to the wife of the experience, the husband might have spared her the trauma he inflicted had he years earlier sought private counseling for help in overcoming his own compulsive sexual behavior. His admitted guilt and unhappiness over that behavior would appear to have been motive enough, but obviously it wasn't. It is unfortunate that so many of us do await a severe crisis before taking initiatives to work creative changes in our marriages. It is, surely, preferable that we take initiatives in the present to help us improve and enliven our relationship now, rather than permit the life to slowly drain out of our marriage or let conditions develop that have the potential for traumatic marital suffering.

Some of those initiatives are relatively simple and in themselves quite enjoyable. Like Ruth and Martin, a couple might take advantage of the family workshops, retreats, and weekends for married couples which nearly all synagogues or churches offer. The Roman Catholic Marriage Encounter Movement—which has since been followed by the Jewish Marriage Experience weekend and the Episcopal Expression of Marriage Encounter—has brought increased joy to nearly a quarter of a million couples at this writing. While religious orientations vary—and attendance at religious services is not compulsory—the weekends follow much the same format. A team composed of a clergyman and a married couple lead the couples in workshop sessions in which they write letters to their partners on certain topics. Then, in private, the couple exchange their letters and dialogue about what they've written. The Marriage Encounter Movement has now spread to forty states and is still growing, primarily because the couples who have been helped by their weekend are eager to share their newfound joy by encouraging others to attend.

The breakthroughs experienced by couples differ for each, but there seem to be few who do not find their relationship renewed as a result of devoting a weekend to such mutual dialoguing about it. Most of the couples continue that dialoguing in their married lives through an exercise called the "Ten and Ten." At some time during the day each takes ten minutes to write a love letter to the other in which feelings about some specific topic—be it God, love, death, sex, their vacation plans, his overtime work—are expressed. Then, later, when they are together, they exchange these letters and spend ten minutes in discussing them.

A similar experience of renewal has been found by couples who involve themselves in the Family Cluster Program, where that is available. This program brings whole families together on a regular basis for projects in common and the sharing of mutual concerns. It is directly concerned with improving the quality of the relationships within families by overcoming the isolation in which all too many families exist today.

Most retreat houses and many churches and synagogues provide evening or weekend programs likewise geared to offering insights and experiences beneficial to married couples. Any couple, no matter how untroubled, can benefit from such programs. In fact, the Marriage Encounter Program is specifically geared for couples who have a relatively healthy, stable marriage relationship, and many of the other programs assume that the couples attending are, at the very least, full of good will toward one another and simply looking for ways to make a good marriage even better.

Utilizing such resources is one means open to all of us to bring new life to our marriages. It has been my privilege to conduct one-day or weekend workshops in which couples married ten, twenty, even thirty-five years have chosen to inform me that they've "never communicated better in years." What was done for them was not esoteric at all: a context was provided in which, with all distractions removed, they could focus totally upon their own relationship and dialogue about it with one another in full privacy on a meaningful level. In short, for the period of time taken by such workshops, the couple have given their marriage relationship central consideration. By experiencing the rewards of doing so, they often permanently restore that relationship to the place of first priority in their lives.

Another aid to re-opening doors to more intimate dialoguing in a marriage is John Drescher's little book *Talking It Over* (Scottdale, Pa: Herald Press, 1975). The book consists of a series of incomplete sentences, such as "I feel closest to you when . . ." and "I feel most alone when . . ." In completing the sentences, they can go at their own pace, stay at their individual levels of comfort on any page, while the book guides them both into a meaningful sharing of personal feelings about themselves, one another, and their marriage. Foregoing the evening television show in order to engage in the sort of dialogue Drescher's book facilitates is a very simple decision, but one which can lead the couple into a newer awareness of and appreciation for each other; rewards not to be gained from any television show.

Dr. Herbert Otto's book, *More Joy in Your Marriage* (Pocket Books, 1971), offers a large variety of ideas and exercises aimed at revitalizing the marital relationship, from which a couple can select those which are appropriate to themselves. Among these is the "brainstorming session." Recognizing that many of the happiest occasions, the memorable events of our marriages were ones that were planned either by one or both of the spouses, the brainstorming session is aimed at coming up with ideas for further marriage-enhancing experiences.

In brainstorming, the initial emphasis is upon getting a series of ideas down on paper, the more the better. In this initial stage each partner simply throws out ideas, however impractical at the moment. No adverse criticism of an idea is permitted. The larger the quantity, the more possibility there is of winnowing out a number of good ones. A good topic for an initial brainstorming session might be "What could we do together that would delight us both?"

The couple produce ideas without restrictions or negative comments. Upon reaching the limits of their imagination in composing their list, they seek to combine those ideas that go together, and to improve upon some of those that with reflection can be made better. With the list now firmed up, the couple then choose from it the five or six ideas that seem to them best in quality and the most practical for fulfillment in the near future. Having done this, the couple take the final step of actually selecting one idea and make specific plans for putting it into action.

Brainstorming has been used for many years by advertising agencies, magazine staffs, "think tank" people, and in various parts of the industrial and business world. I have had occasion to follow Dr. Otto's lead in applying this technique to marriage during my workshops, and I have found that the participants not only enjoy the process of brainstorming itself, but the follow-up evaluation of the workshops show that the couples who acted upon their ideas were very glad they did. This is another example of how a little time (the whole process may take less than an hour) and some creative thinking applied to the marriage can build more pleasure for the couple.

Aside from mutually conceived plans for "occasions of

delight," individual spouses can arrange such occasions for each other. That marriage in which the partners are accustomed to applying their imaginations to the creative task of surprising the spouse with some token of love is a marriage that shows signs of life. We might ask ourselves when we last did something that showed our spouse the truly special place he or she holds in our life. All of us need the feeling of being loved; all of us like to be appreciated; all of us want to be considered very special to someone. Yet, the feeling of being taken for granted is a common one in many marriages. Expressions of endearment, when used at all, no longer have the ring of authenticity because they've slipped into a simple part of the daily vocabulary, are said without full weight given them. ("Love, will you take out the garbage?" "Nice meal, honey.")

All too often, gift-giving has been restricted to the commercially advertised holidays, birthdays, or anniversaries. In a sense, such gifts are slightly tarnished tokens of love, for, after all, one is expected to give something on those days; it's customary. A husband or wife taking the time to plan a surprise, to fulfill a wish, to choose a special present, can turn what is but another ordinary day into an "occasion" of its own. The lack of expectedness itself adds luster to the gift, for its motivation is more clearly seen as the desire to express appreciation for the other, to bring unexpected joy to the other.

The gifts given do not have to be bought in a store. They might be the gift of breakfast in bed or the reading of a love poem. Whatever form the inspiration provides, the message is love. Like the symbolism of the sexual act itself, which at its best is an act of a loving couple that shows forth their love and at the same time makes more love, so the other signs and symbols that we offer to one another do not only demonstrate the love felt, they help to further its growth. That is why even the simplest gestures of love have a way of flowering forth in surprising reciprocity. That, too, is why we ought not wait until we are feeling especially affectionate to provide such tokens of our love. Indeed, the arid days of the relationship, the times when intimacy seems to have ebbed, are special times for taking loving initiatives, even in small ways, which quicken the spirit of the other and provide emotional nourishment to the relationship. It is precisely those times of tension between us, those times when our personal intimacy is in danger of being lost, when we are called upon to actualize our potentiality for greater loving.

A common source of tensions in the marital relationship is the lack of true freedom in the sexual expression of love. The bodily expression of love is not something that "just happens" to be mutually pleasurable or a source of frustration. Whether it is a spiritually and emotionally enriching experience or a source of worry and even alienation is something very much, if not entirely, the creation of the husband and wife.

Some have settled for a routinized sexual pattern which not only does not enrich them, but nourishes a sense of disappointment that sex hasn't fulfilled its promises. Even if they aren't embittered or frustrated, they do not know the pleasures of sexual activity that are truly expressive of their desire for unity, for spontaneous freedom. Just as the totality of their relationship's quality reveals itself in their sexual life, so does the sexual dialogue color their daily lives.

Many couples seem willing to put time and energies into work and housekeeping and gardening chores, or to discuss thoroughly their vacation plans, and yet they somehow expect the quality of their sexual activities to take care of itself, to improve without their own creative efforts. It is not atypical to enter a home and find an entire shelf of cookbooks in the kitchen, a row of books relating to his profession or their hobbies in the parlor or study, and not a single work on sex anywhere on the premises. Yet the enhancement of the sexual joy of the couple depends greatly upon their willingness to be accurately informed about sexual matters, to be more comfortable in open discussions about their feelings and thoughts about sex.

Disappointment with the sexual relationship need not be

endured for long by anyone. It is in itself a sign of the need on the part of the couple to put some time, some creative energy, into mutual education about this important aspect of their relationship. For them to do so—especially when this means the sometimes painful wrenching away from the chains of parentally imposed inhibitions and the stripping away of masks currently being worn—is an act of love. It speaks of a willingness to undergo such growing pains for the sake of the beloved, for the sake of enriching the pleasure and the joy of their union in love.

Sometimes a book can be of help if mutually read and discussed. The couple may dialogue more comfortably about sexual matters through the discussion of an author's remarks. Thus, the agreement or disagreement about one point or another is directed at the author and not at one another. Such mutual reading, as well as providing factual information that may be extremely helpful, offers insights into one another's reaction to the options opened up by the authors that can build toward a growing freedom of discussion and action in matters sexual.

Some sexual problems cannot be worked out by the couple as a couple. Impotency or consistent premature ejaculation, the problem of the woman who never has an orgasm, and other severe forms of sexual dysfunction, require that the partners seek competent outside help. Not all counselors are equally helpful; the telephone directory is the last place to seek a therapist. Nor is it wise simply to walk into the nearest clinic. One of the better ways of assuring that we get competent help is to ask one's clergyman for a recommendation. He usually is in a position to know something of the results accomplished by those to whom he has referred people. It is also possible that another couple who have been aided by therapy can offer the name of their counselor. The local office of the Psychological Association usually has a referral service that can be called for advice about those professionals best suited to deal with the specific problem. The reason for such caution is that the counseling field is not without its aberrant practitioners. But this

note of caution should not delay anyone from seeking sexual therapy who needs it. There are now about 3500 clinics
in the United States dealing with the most severe sorts of
sexual dysfunction, and they have a very good record of
success. There is no longer any lack of help available to
those suffering sexual dysfunction.

It is during the critical hours or days of a marriage that
the spiritual resources of the spouses are called upon. It
may be that the crisis is a minor one; feelings have been
hurt during a quarrel, something unimportant in itself has
become a source of injury. The natural desire is to withdraw entirely, to nurse one's wounds, to close in upon
oneself, and in one way or another "punish" the other,
perhaps through the silent treatment or by being sullen
and uncooperative. It may be that the hurt has been severe
—the sort of blow experienced by the wife whose husband
revealed his many infidelities and asked for a divorce—and
the injured party would have every reason for feeling that
a mortal blow has been struck at the relationship. Every
fiber of one's being screams out that a gross injustice has
been perpetrated; the desire to see the other suffer for the
wrong done is purely natural. Who would blame such a wife
for steeling herself against such a husband, taking him "to
the cleaners" via the divorce court.

Much can depend upon the spiritual resources of the
couple. Those who have only a "daily" view of life, whose
vision does not go beyond the compass of the natural, are
more easily led by their emotions along the path of "hard-
ening their hearts" toward the other in the smaller as well
as the larger moments of hurt. And, by doing so in the
smaller matters, they create a marital climate conducive to
major storms.

A couple who have nourished a larger vision of life, and
who are able to draw upon their religious faith, can draw
strength from that conviction. The darkness that has
clouded their marriage, the pain they are now going
through, is no less dark, no less painful than that of people
who do not share their religious convictions. Their beliefs,
however, keep them from feeling alone in their struggle

against the darkness and the pain. In their prayer/dialogue with God, they seek His guidance through the valley of darkness, trust His love to help them redeem the time. Their conviction that their decisions and actions have significance beyond the immediate moment often enables them to show responses to a situation in a way beyond the "natural" response. It may be their awareness of the redemptive value of suffering that sustains them; it may be their decision to live out the call to love one's enemies (and what is the spouse at such a time but an enemy?); it may be the realization that forgiveness is an essential ingredient of loving, both human and divine; it may be any one of dozens of possible insights which prompt in them the action that affords the moment of reconciliation brought about by a loving response of one to the other.

The response made during the times when loving may be made difficult most clearly distinguishes the living marriage from the marriage that has become a mere living arrangement. In the latter, the couple may be functioning, but estrangement has been allowed to become the pattern of the relationship. Because they do not actively work to recreate the situation, do not put energies into change, their marriage is a "still life"; increased pleasure, deeper intimacy, emotional growth do not occur. In a living marriage, however, the couple see their times of estrangement as occasions calling for their loving in a truer, less selfish way. They view conflicts as challenges to deeper understanding of one another. They know that the price of true freedom with one another, freedom to be themselves together, freedom from the sense of personal alienation which afflicts us, is actively pursuing the goal of closer unity, opening themselves up in affirmation of the other, accepting the other's affirmations of themselves. If wounds have been received, they are aware that forgiveness is the form that love then assumes. If they have wounded the other, they know that the first aid to be delivered is the acknowledgment of fault and that the healing arts include the words, "I'm sorry," and the increased application of tender, loving care.

The couple whose emotional bond aspires to such quality do not segregate their sexual lovemaking out of the totality of their lives together, but see it as another facet of the same reality: their mutual commitment to love one another to fuller life. Signs of physical affection, the hand on the arm, the embrace of welcome, the sensuous massage, spoon-fashion cuddling for sleep, the sexual act itself, are but further expressions of their commitment to one another, and at the same time increase their enjoyment of life together. Their life is but a continuum of deepening intimacy, greater self-knowledge, increased knowledge of the other, mutual growth in humanity. Their acceptance of each other grows more unconditional as their intimacy grows; their respect for one another's differences, their sensitivity to one another's needs, their trust in one another's love, increases as together they face the trials of daily life. The years test and prove the quality of their commitment and each victory—of love over selfishness—makes them that much stronger to meet the next problem, the next trial.

The couple involved in a marriage like this are the truly liberated couple. Their mutual love has driven out the fear that enslaves: the fear of betrayal, the fear of rejection, the fear of being found inadequate by the one we love. To paraphrase the Gospel passage: they have laid down their lives and they have found fuller life. They made a profound commitment to one another and, far from losing their freedom, they find themselves liberated from their isolation, freed to live a life of loving and being loved. Living not only with but for one another, they can discover the power of love not only to encourage and enliven the beloved but to bring delight and increased joy of life to the lover.

Not that any of the couples in living marriages might describe themselves in this fashion, for most know that it is fruitless to try to articulate the realities of the mystery in which they live. They do, however, have in common that appreciation of the mystery of marriage, if by mystery we mean that which is beyond the capture of words, cannot be defined once and for all, cannot have its meaning exhausted in descriptive phrases. If such couples stumble over definitions of love, it is not because they have too little experience of love, but because they have known authentic loving and know that no single definition encapsulates it. If they find difficulty describing the goodness, the truth, and the beauty of their relationship, it is because their very tangible experience of these is something they know words cannot adequately convey to another.

There is a calm at the center of the life of such a couple. It is a tranquillity of spirit borne of the acceptance of themselves and of each other that is unquestioned; there is no doubting their total commitment to their relationship, whatever may befall them. Some superficial observers would mistake this calm, this peace-full-ness that is at the heart of the true marriage relationship, for a lack of excitement, a lack of sense of adventure. These are the ones who call such marriages dull. But it is out of that very calm center, out of that sense of security, that the couple in a living marriage experience a fullness of ecstasy that cannot be the portion of the insecure, the threatened, the uncommitted, the manipulators, and the self-seekers. For it is only possible to give oneself fully away to the other when one has fullest confidence in oneself and in the other.

We earlier defined ecstasy as "being beside oneself." In a living marriage each has grown in an appreciation of their unity as a couple to such a point that they are always in a state of "being beside oneself," for the other is appreciated as another "self"; what is done for the other is done for oneself, too; what hurts the other, causes oneself pain; what delights the other, brings delight to the self. Here is part of the clue to the "two-in-one-flesh-ness" of marriage. Neither loses his or her identity or personality, but each has an experience of the two-in-one-ness, of the "we" that transcends the "me" and the "you." For each, the experience of life is enlarged because each is not only himself, but is also "beside himself" in the person of the spouse and can see the world through the other's eyes as well; can experience existence through the spouse's sensibilities as well as his own.

Nor does the outflow cease there. The living marriage, by being what it is—a lived-out love commitment—is revelatory to a troubled society, in which alienation is commonplace, that community is possible. It announces to the alienated that love is not a dream. To those whose personal experiences have brought them to the edge of despair, it is a sign of hope. To those who have been wounded by their bewildered wanderings in the contemporary sexual wilderness, it offers an appreciation of the fact that fidelity is not only possible, but is the fertile soil for the full flowering of sexual loving. It accomplishes this by merely being what it is: a living marriage.

But beyond the sign value of being what it is in today's world, the living marriage manifests itself in the partners' mutual concern for the world about them. A few decades ago it was commonplace for writers on marriage, especially religiously oriented ones, to warn couples against the "egoism of the two," against the marriage closed in upon itself in some sort of mutual idolatry. In my opinion those warnings were unnecessary. In the first place, mutual idolatry cannot survive for very long in any marriage, for the humanity of the partners all too rapidly becomes apparent to them both. Secondly, the marriage that is created by the partners to be a vital and vitalizing relationship is a veritable education in being more fully human. The partners are aiding one another to grow into full personhood, to exercise their own best talents as persons. That very growth has called out of each of them a deepened sense of personal responsibility, a spirit of self-sacrifice, an enhanced ability to love, to experience compassion, to communicate themselves generously. The days of gladness they've shared have worked to the increase of their faith, their hope, their love. The very marriage relationship that has made them more fully human beings leads them to open the doors of their domicile to those in need of help. It also leads them to go out through those same doors to that larger, broken world so much in need of persons whose very life style upholds the message of life and love.

SUGGESTED READINGS

Bach, George and Wyden, Peter. *The Intimate Enemy: How To Fight Fair in Love and Marriage.* New York: Avon Books, 1968.

> A compendium of information on interpersonal communications problems and how to overcome them. No one needs everything in this book, but everyone can find something of help in improving their own personal dialogue.

Berne, Eric. *Sex in Human Loving.* New York: Pocket Books, 1971.

> The author of "Games People Play" wittily and wisely offers insights into our sexual relationships. He draws upon his transactional analysis approach to human relations to show us why we're so often playing unsatisfying "games" here, too, and how to stop doing so.

Brothers, Joyce. *The Brothers System for Liberated Love and Marriage.* New York: Avon Books, 1972.

> Primarily directed to a female readership, this book can be of help to both men and women in taking practical action to enhance their relationship.

Comfort, Alex, ed. *The Joy of Sex: A Gourmet Guide to Love Making.* New York: Crown Publishers, Inc., 1972.

> Perhaps the ultimate contemporary "sex manual," but one which generally avoids the mechanistic approach and stresses love—because "you don't get high-quality sex on any other basis." Lavishly illustrated, it offers information and options which might help some couples employ more creative imagination in their own lovemaking.

Delderfield, R. F. *Mr. Sermon.* New York: Pocket Books, 1971.

> A novel about a middle-aged man who makes a dramatic break with his present, leaving job, wife, and children to

find freedom. What he discovers and what he rediscovers constitute the story. Like all good fiction, this novel offers us truths about ourselves. Mr. Sermon's journey may make us more capable of handling our own middle-age crisis without having to run away from home.

Drescher, John. *Talking It Over.* Scottdale, Pa.: Herald Press, 1975.

This small book is not for reading but for using. It is designed to foster more intimate dialoguing between husband and wife. When thoughtfully used, it can do just that.

Inkeles, Gordon and Todris, Murray. *The Art of Sensual Massage.* San Francisco: Straight Arrow Books, 1972.

Amply illustrated by photographs by Robert Foothorap, this book is designed not only for reading but for using— as a guide to nonverbal, physical communication of love through bringing into play the delights of touching and being touched.

Le Shan, Eda. *The Wonderful Crisis of Middle Age.* New York: Warner Paperback Library, 1974.

Subtitled "Some Personal Reflections," this is a remarkably stimulating and encouraging book by a wife and mother who is also a professional in family-life matters. It is a commonsense, hope-full book of value to anyone wanting to "continue to explore the astonishment of living."

Masters, William H. and Johnson, Virginia E. (in association with Robert Levin). *The Pleasure Bond: A New Look at Sexuality and Commitment.* Boston: Little, Brown and Co., 1974.

The most authoritative experts on human sexuality in our time examine some of the destructive side of the "sexual revolution" and offer counsel aimed at helping persons intensify their own "pleasure bond."

Otto, Herbert A. *More Joy in Your Marriage.* New York: Pocket Books, 1971.

A wide-ranging compendium of ideas and practical exercises for "developing your marriage potential." Any couple should be able to find some things in this book that will lead to enhancement of their marriage, work some changes, bring them more pleasure, or even joy

Reuben, David. *Everything You Always Wanted to Know About Sex (but were afraid to ask)*. New York: David McKay, 1970.

Now also available in paperback, this book is written in a breezy question-and-answer style and seeks to respond to the need for basic information on all the physical aspects of sex.

DATE DUE

Also by Clayton C. Barbeau

Delivering the Male

**Out of the Tough-Guy Trap
into a Better Marriage**

This challenging, empathetic book about men (for *men and women*) addresses the shifting, often disturbing reality of what it means to be a man in today's world. Barbeau explores the tough-guy mystique's failure to produce satisfying personhood and fulfillment. And he outlines positive steps for achieving greater freedom, enjoyment, and a deeper "at-homeness" that can be found in a less restrictive, more sensitive and tender male role.

ISBN: 0-86683-642-X